A YEAR IN BAGHDAD

A Year in Baghdad

JOAN BAEZ, SR.

AND

ALBERT V. BAEZ

Illustrations by Joan Baez

JOHN DANIEL & COMPANY · SANTA BARBARA · 1988

.988 by Joan Baez, Sr. and Albert V. Baez

ations copyright ©1988 by Joan Baez

ALL RIGHTS RESERVED
PRINTED IN THE UNITED STATES OF AMERICA

Design and typography by Jim Cook
SANTA BARBARA, CALIFORNIA

LIBRARY OF CONGRESS CATALOGING-IN-PUBLICATION DATA
Baez, Joan, 1913-
A year in Baghdad / Joan Baez, Sr. & Albert V. Baez.
ISBN 0-936784-38-5 (PBK.) $9.95
1. Baghdad (Iraq)—Description.   2. Baez, Joan, 1913-
3. Baez, A.V.   4. Baez family.   5. Wives—United States—Biography
6. Physicists—United States—Biography.   I. Baez, A.V.
II. Title.
DS79.9.B25B32 1988   88-11721
915.67′4—dc 19   CIP

Published by
JOHN DANIEL & COMPANY
POST OFFICE BOX 21922
SANTA BARBARA, CALIFORNIA 93121

To Jeanne Kamal, good friend
whose candle never failed to brighten up the darkest hours.
With love, Joan

To Naseeb Dajani, whose life led me to respect Islam.
Al

Table of Contents

Foreword

Mimi Fariña

I STILL SEE SCENES from the school bus window: men squatting on street corners with their robes wrapped around their legs; women walking with great packages on their heads, their black robes billowing as one anklet jingled with their straight-spined step. I remember my own walks to and from the schoolbus . . . stepping in my sister Pauline's footprints in the dust, small brown shoes making smaller prints within hers, so I'd grow up to be just like her. A row of pills at the head of Joanie's bed as she lay ill and weak with hepatitis. The family venturing out in a group, Pops always with camera, Mother's linen hankie smelling of Chanel No. 5. A dead horse floating in the Tigris River, men who whipped their skinny work donkeys to the point of collapse on the street, people throwing rocks at dogs and cats, beggars filthy and empty-eyed. The brown dusty air by day and beautiful starlit sky by night; the mosquito net that kept huge bugs from jumping on us when we slept outside on hot nights; the small room where I woke crying because I couldn't remember how much of the earth was water and how much land, and where England and America were on the globe for my test the next day; mother's soothing words and hand-written notes to Sister Rose, who read them aloud to the entire class. Sister Rose, her pink puffy cheeks squeezed into her starched nun's hat, her heavy black dress that rustled as she passed your desk, her black, stubby Tom McAnns teaching us the five positions of ballet from beneath her floor-length habit.

Gone were the milk-and-cookie breaks of kindergarten at home, the easy nap time, the white paste that tasted so good off wooden rules; gone was Professor Woolie, our pet collie; my baton and the satin and velvet dress that Mrs. Santa had made for me the year before. Gone were the crayons and dolls. Baghdad was an abrupt change in pace for the entire family.

In the following pages, my mother and father skillfully reveal some of their memories of the nine months our family spent in Iraq. Both parents wrote their personal chapters without consulting each other, and the two stories were then woven together by their publisher. I had no idea how vivid and full (not to mention humorous) their descriptions would be, and I am honored to encourage you, dear reader, to enjoy the details of one family's journey into a very foreign land.

Mimi   Joanie   Pauline   Popsy   Mummy   Smudge

Prologue

Al and Joan

THE SCREEN DOOR slapped shut as I entered the living room of our house in Redlands, California. It was another of those clear spring days in 1951 that made the contrast between warm Redlands and cold Buffalo so gratifying.

Joan greeted me with a kiss. She had an envelope in her hand. "You have a letter from Paris," she said. "I'm terribly curious."

I recognized the Unesco logo on the blue airmail envelope and felt a surge of excitement as I ripped it open. I read selected portions of it out loud: "The purpose of this letter is to inquire if you would be interested in serving as a visiting professor of physics on the faculty of science in Baghdad, Iraq."

Joan's eyes lit up. "Baghdad!" she exclaimed. "You mean the *Thousand and One Nights* Baghdad? How exciting!" Then, with a quizzical look, "Just where *is* Baghdad? And how come they're inviting *you* to come?"

Up to that point in my career my travels had been confined pretty much to the Western hemisphere. I could not have told you precisely where Baghdad was in Iraq, nor where Iraq was in the Middle East. I harbored the vague sort of ideas about Baghdad that most of us have who have been charmed in childhood by tales of Ali Baba and the Forty Thieves. It conjured up distant visions of bazaars, mosques, calls to prayer, and veiled women.

We looked up Baghdad in the *Encyclopedia Britannica* and I reminded Joan that I had written Unesco from Buffalo about a year earlier asking if they had any openings for a physicist.

At that time I was working at the Cornell Aeronautical Laboratory in Buffalo. Sev Chapman had hired me as an experimental physicist. We had taught physics together at Stanford. After all those years working for a Ph.D. and getting slave wages as a teaching assistant I was now earning a respectable salary which enabled us to buy all those things our family had done without while I was a graduate student—a car, a new refrigerator, a piano, a stereo.

Although I had been hired as a physicist, they had made me the leader of an operations research group working on a classified project dealing with the defense of the U.S. fleet against air attack. Before accepting that assignment I had asked Sev what operations research was and he had said: "We don't know either, but we know it's important and physicists have been instrumental in its development. We want you to find out what it's all about and tell us if you think it is relevant to the work of this lab."

And that's how I found myself, one bleak and cold winter morning in 1950, in a bunk on the aircraft carrier *Coral Sea* in the Caribbean. It carried the admiral of Operation Portex, one of the largest peace-time amphibious operations.

The prospects were at once exciting, challenging and disturbing. I had never used my talents on war-related work before. I had thought vaguely about using science for peace, but I was no pacifist. Here was a chance to do something big, exciting and possibly useful in the defense of our country, and, in the process, get well paid for doing it! I experienced for the first time the lure of power.

But a feeling of uneasiness enveloped me. Against my wishes and my better judgment, I was being drawn deeper into war-related work. My concern had begun several years earlier when we all learned that nuclear weapons had been invented and engineered by physicists and that some of them had even promoted their deployment.

As I lay in my bunk I made back-of-the-envelope estimates of the cost of Operation Portex. The hardware alone came to hundreds of millions of dollars. It involved several carriers and their brand new jet planes, each costing about half a million dollars, as well as many destroyers and other ships all outfitted with the newest electronic communication and control gear. For the first time in my life I began pondering in earnest the effectiveness of military force in achieving peace.

I read an article in the Sunday *New York Times* about a new United Nations organization—Unesco—whose aim was to promote peace through education, science, and culture. I was moved by the words of the preamble of its Constitution: "Since wars begin in the minds of men, it is in the minds of men that the defenses of peace must be constructed." The wish to use my knowledge of science for constructive ends began to develop. Doing research in military operations didn't seem to be the right approach.

Knowing that I was disturbed about my role at the Cornell lab, Joan suggested we attend a meeting of the Society of Friends in Buffalo. She had graduated from Oakwood, a Quaker school, and knew of the Quaker peace testimony. There I was introduced for the first time to the words George Fox addressed to King Charles II in 1660: "We utterly deny all outward wars and strife, and fighting with outward weapons, for any end or pretense whatever, this is our testimony to the whole world." I also read the Epistle of London Yearly Meeting in 1804, which stated: "We feel bound explicitly to avow our continued unshaken persuasion that all war is utterly incompatible with the plain precepts of our Divine Lord and Lawgiver ... who hath said 'Love your enemies.'"

My conversion to pacifism, which was to take several years, was probably born on the aircraft carrier *Coral Sea* and in the silence of the Buffalo Meeting of the Religious Society of Friends. Before finishing even one year at the Cornell lab I had made up my mind that research for the military was not for me.

I wrote to Unesco in Paris offering my services, and I applied for a teaching job at the University of Redlands in California.

"Oh, Popsy, let's go back to California" was the plea from Pauline, Joanie, and Mimi. Joan's entreaty was more reserved: "I'd love to go back, but you are the bread-winner and I'll accept whatever you decide." But I knew that she too longed to get back to the sunshine. She hated the cold and drizzle of Buffalo.

So I accepted the Redlands offer and we moved to our bungalow-style home on Campus Avenue in Redlands after only one year in Buffalo. We loved Redlands. In her beloved garden Joan could smile again. The girls made friends quickly. They romped on the lawn and climbed the huge avocado tree in our back yard. We seemed to be settling in for a long and pleasant haul.

But in the middle of the school year this letter from Unesco came in out of the blue. I had almost forgotten I had written to them the previous year. And now they were offering me a job. I read some more to Joan: "The Government of Iraq has asked us for a professor of physics for the Faculty of Science on a year's appointment, and we would like to know whether you would be interested in having your name submitted as a candidate for this position.

"The main function of the post is to organize teaching at university level of physics and to initiate research.

"Unesco will pay the cost of transportation to Iraq and return for you and your family."

When I brought the subject up at the dinner table I was deluged with questions. Joanie said, "You mean we would all get to fly to Baghdad?"

I had obviously stirred up some interest. "That's right," I said. "With stopovers in places like New York, Paris, and Beirut."

"But we've only been in Redlands about six months," said Pauline, the voice of caution and reason. This was true, of course, and I worried about that too. Would I always be flitting about from one place to the next? What would President

Armacost think? He would have to grant me leave of absence after spending only one school year at the university.

I talked to Joan after meeting with President Armacost. A lesser man would have balked and reminded me that it was unfair to leave after having just arrived. He was magnanimous enough to concede the possibility that this would be an enriching experience for me. He may also have hoped that his compliance would generate a sense of loyalty and dedication to Redlands when I returned.

"Don't forget, Al, just one year!"

I sprouted wings of joy and flew out of his office.

The prospects of the impending Unesco mission had idealistic claims on my conscience. Believing that the constructive work of Unesco held the seeds of future peace, I felt that I had a definite opportunity to implement with actions what had been, until then, merely idealistic dreams. I also felt the lure of travel to exotic places.

WE HAD THE summer to do what had to be done, including passport pictures, eighteen inoculations each (a lot of sore arms), and wardrobes to find in the second-hand shops. We had to keep reminding ourselves to think on the positive side; this would be an adventure.

It was not surprising that enthusiasm was low. We had moved so many times while the girls were little. Mimi said, "Can we take the costume box?" She and her friends all but lived in great bustles and busts. Spent their time parading up and down the sidewalks being ladies. Of course she'd like to take the precious box.

Joanie's first thought was her beautiful collie dog, still a woolly pup. "Will I have to leave Mr. Wooly?" She was willing, but sad about it. She loved animals.

Pauline loved them, too. Her choice was horses. She drew them, wandered about the house on all fours with her friends, whinnying; most of all she loved to ride. All three girls were having a summer of riding lessons. "I guess that's the end of riding," she said. She added later, "We already had Baghdad in

13

ancient history, Mum." It seemed that was enough to put any young person off.

We were moving right along with our plans when Pauline's skin turned a strange yellow. There were light yellow finger spots on her face. Then one day she doubled up with pain.

The diagnosis was hepatitis. The doctor said *hospital*. We went immediately. Pauline had not told us that she threw up her breakfast every day and sometimes she could hardly walk because of the pains. She didn't want to miss the horseback riding.

A week later I recognized the sulfur-like odor on Mimi's breath. She joined Pauline in the hospital. Now we must revamp our traveling plans.

Al had to be in Paris to be briefed early in August. To me, the word "brief" always sounded as if underwear had to be inspected. Whatever it meant, we had only two weeks.

The plan was to have Joanie go to Paris with Popsy and we'd join them a month later. Joanie was now excited. She couldn't stop bouncing. Going to Paris alone with Popsy! Her eyes stayed so wide open that I was afraid they'd snap if she blinked.

When I left the two of them at the heliport, Al looked anxious. I knew he was worried about leaving us. "They'll be fine," I said. "Good doctors, good hospital, and we'll see you at Orly Airport in one month." I swallowed something square in my throat as I hugged them, then watched them climb into the helicopter.

In three weeks, Pauline and Mimi were uncontrollably well. I could hear their shrill laughter at the far end of the corridor when I entered the hospital. They had pillow fights, blew water through their straws, rode horsey on the bed rails.

The nurses were far too polite when I asked them how the girls were. "Oh, they're doing fine," one of the nurses would say. "We're so proud of them." But I knew that it would be a huge relief when they waved a final goodbye.

Another week, and the early morning sun caught us sitting in our jet-assist prop plane, the girls' adrenaline high, by the look of Mimi's legs swinging back and forth like a couple of miniature baseball bats. Her braids slapped her back as she turned her head this way and that to see everything. A Dramamine each and we were soon watching the relief map below us disappear while we climbed between the strawberry clouds into the early morning blue.

Having traveled by plane only once before, on a short and wild stormy flight, I took care to read the pamphlets and diagrams that told us what to do in an emergency. I started to plan my strategy, noting that the girls were already sleeping when my entire body finally relaxed. Everything was in good order and I fell asleep to the rhythm of the motors.

It was all easy until we saw no familiar faces at Orly Airport and I had to try my French. Pauline waited, wide-eyed and motionless beside our wall of luggage. Mimi felt sick and dropped on a bench. I lunged for a stewardess who was disappearing behind the next exit. "S'il vous plait, Madame, voulez-vous—call this number?" My knees and my voice trembled together.

She understood, called the number. There was no answer. She hung up. "Respond-pas. C'est dommage," she twitted, and was gone.

Now what? Then I saw two familiar brown legs double-timing it under a green coat. I knew those legs, and I knew that face and the tanned one behind it. They were here! We were here! For a moment my knees wobbled. Then a round of hugs. A good blow on my handkerchief took care of my motherly emotions. Now Al would take over. I wished I could be so steady and capable.

For a couple of weeks we lived luxuriously in a small apartment in the shadow of the Eiffel Tower. The maid brought us breakfast in bed—hot chocolate, café au lait. It smelled so good. She brought heated plates with brioches, croissants, sweet butter, and delicious jams. "We must enjoy this, you guys," I said. "God knows how it will all be next week at this time." We were excited about getting to Baghdad now.

While Al worked at Unesco House in Paris, Joanie guided the rest of us through the nearby parks with warnings about rules,

"Never walk on the grass. The police shout at you. They're nasty. Don't sit on a chair unless you have ten francs, because the old woman with the black bag will scream at you. She's nasty too. You can ride up the elevator in Unesco House, but you have to walk down. Ask for 'le cabinet,' when you have to go to the bathroom. They laugh at you when you say 'toilette.' And always say 'bonjour' to Fernandel." She knelt down and gave Fernandel, the German shepherd who guarded all of Unesco, a smothering hug.

At last, early one morning, we were off in a taxi to the airport and Middle East Airlines. Flight number 073, like a camel in the sky, rocked, dipped, and lunged through the sizzling air, over the vast desert, over the tiny mud-hut villages, each one shimmering like a mirage from the intense heat. Think of it! We were almost in Baghdad!

Baghdad Arrival

Al

OUR FIRST REAL taste of this strange new world came when we boarded the Middle East Airlines DC-3 in Beirut with destination Baghdad. We were among the few passengers in Western attire. Almost all the others wore the characteristic robes and *abayahs* of the Arab world. The turbanned men twiddled their prayer beads and gawked at my girls. The women peeked at them through a tiny aperture in their veils. It was unbelievably hot, noisy and smelly.

Before long we were flying over the junction of the Tigris and Euphrates rivers, starting to make our descent into Baghdad. As the noise of the engines diminished I could imagine I was really flying down into the city of the thousand and one nights on a magic carpet. But inside the plane we were hot and apprehensive as the mud-colored houses of Baghdad, then a city of half a million people, came into view.

Each girl carried her maroon TWA bag with her personal belongings. We stood in the aisle waiting for the airplane door to open. Fatigue, heat, and fear made speech impossible. We hoped that opening the door of the plane would bring relief. We were not prepared for what actually happened—a veritable implosion. A blast of hot air as from an oven surged into the plane when the door was finally opened. The thought of walking out into that inferno struck terror in our hearts. We were caught in a stream of humanity pushing to get out. The heat caused us to wince. It was difficult to see.

Professor Mohler, who had flown in the day before, was at the airport to meet us. He looked at us in our bedraggled state and kept shaking his head back and forth. When he got close to me he said: "*Im*possible, *im*possible. This is no place for a Western woman. I'll never be able to bring my wife here."

Two Jesuit priests in white robes were also there to greet us. They had read of our impending arrival in the English language newspaper. Father Connell's face radiated warmth and friendship. He was the director of Baghdad College, the Jesuit school for boys. I will never forget Father Connell because of this gesture of welcome and because he was from Brooklyn and sounded like it. Father Connell got a taxi for us and as we parted he said, "You must come to visit Baghdad College. We have a good physics teaching laboratory. You will like it!"

We dragged ourselves through the corridor of the Semiramis Hotel, oblivious of everything except the heat. We were shown to a large high-ceilinged room with paint peeling off the walls. There was no air conditioning—only one large four-bladed ceiling fan which simply circulated hot air from one part of the room to another. We plunked ourselves down on the beds, exhausted. I made a rough estimate of what each turn of that blade was costing me and I couldn't sleep.

After a few hours of tossing and turning we were hot, bored, restless, and curious to explore our new surroundings. We ventured into the open corridor. The sun had set but it was still oppressively hot. We decided to risk a walk out of our hotel and into Rashid Street. It was the only paved street in Baghdad and ran parallel to the Tigris River.

The impact was devastating. Our senses were outraged. The heat was oppressive, the smells overpowering and the noise of the traffic on Rashid Street unbearable. Our little family group presented an unusual sight on a street where the human population was predominantly male. The few women who ventured forth were covered from head to foot with the black abayah. A solitary male accompanied by four women in short and colorful California dresses was just too much for the Arabs sitting in the open-air tea houses along Rashid Street. They couldn't keep their eyes off mother Joan, Pauline (12), Joanie (10) and Mimi (6). Even I felt the pressure of their stares. We decided to brave the new world and walk together on Rashid Street as far as the new bridge.

The din was unbelievable. Many of the taxis kept their horns sounding continuously. They accomplished this by short-circuiting the bare wires that led to the horn button. Every sense was overburdened. New and strange sensations impinged upon our eyes and ears, but the most outrageous in their novelty and severity were the smells. Mix together the vapors emanated by automobiles, camels, donkeys, and sweating men at the end of a scorching hot day and you get a gaseous brew which settles down near the ground out of sheer weight and malice.

We were like the particles of smoke in Brownian Motion bombarded continuously on all sides. A donkey, relieving itself out of several orifices at once and walking briskly along the sidewalk prodded by blows from a stick, banged into me, and I almost fell onto the gooey mess he had produced in the dirt below. The men in Baghdad were in the habit of clearing their throats and spitting indiscriminately into the street, unmindful of the passerby who might become the target of their aqueous missiles which added to the slipperiness of the ground below.

Joan held Mimi and Pauline by the hand. Joanie held my hand, although it was obvious from our grimaces that we would all have preferred to use our hands to hold our noses as we walked.

We reached the bridge only three blocks away. It felt as if we had walked three miles. We decided we had had enough for one day so we turned back and fought our way back to the hotel against a relentless tide of humanity and fumes.

We were relieved to return to the relatively clean and quiet atmosphere of our hotel room. We didn't speak. We just looked at one another. We were all thinking the same thing: "How are we ever going to take this for a whole week, let alone a year?"

Perhaps Professor Mohler had been right at the airport: "*Im*possible, *im*possible" — he always put the emphasis on the first syllable—"No Western woman can survive here." Baghdad was very much a man's world.

Exhausted, we flopped back onto our beds. What else could we do? After about an hour we could see through our tiny windows that it was dark outside. We walked to the rear of the hotel, whose yard bordered on the river. The dry banks of the river Tigris were about twenty feet below us. We could see scavengers at work looking for useful scraps.

Soon the waiters began bringing tables out on the lawn and setting them for dinner. The little colored electric light bulbs that were strung around the yard were lit and the place began to take on a different aspect. Before long visitors from the hotel came out to sit at the tables and order drinks before dinner. Some of them were sheiks who wore flowing robes and elegant turbans. We were famished and the smell of food whetted our appetites. We too sat down and ordered. We watched and were watched.

This was our first introduction to the magic transformation that takes place between day and night in Baghdad. At night, under the light of the tiny colored lamps, all the dirt and the imperfections in the fences and the lawn were invisible. The stars shone with uncommon brilliance. A subtle breeze cooled us off and we were transported to a different world. It would not have surprised us now if the original Ali Baba had appeared.

As we sat there waiting for our meal to be served a tall man with a strongly Semitic face approached us. He had a nose like a pear, elephantine ears, and eyes that squinted so that you could hardly see them.

"Excuse me," he said in a very British accent. "Are you Professor Baez?"

"Yes, I am."

"I am Doctor Ali Kamal. I read about you in the *Iraqi Times*. I presume these are members of your family?"

"Yes. This is Mrs. Baez and these are Pauline, Joan, and Mimi."

"I am very happy to meet you because I have two young daughters and they will be flying in from England with my wife very soon. My wife Jeanne and I met in Oxford, where I did my medical studies."

Thus not Ali Baba but Ali Kamal entered our lives. He waved to an acquaintance sitting at another table and invited him to join us. We noticed that there were no women present except the members of our family. Ali's friend was an Iraqi doctor who seemed very curious about me and my family.

"Are these your daughters?" he asked.

"Yes, they are. Does this surprise you?"

"Well, frankly, yes. You seem too young to be their father. Would you mind telling me your age?"

"I'm thirty-nine."

He looked surprised. "You look much younger." He then looked around and saw two other friends sitting at their tables and waved to them to come over to ours. They were all Iraqi medical doctors. As they finished their meals they came and joined us. They examined me and asked where I had found the fountain of youth. It came as a surprise to me and to my whole family that I should be considered a rare and youthful specimen.

Soon the food was served. It smelled good. Lots of rice and lamb. A variety of sauces and butter—it was called *ghee*—with a peculiar smell. We stayed clear of leafy vegetables; but Ali, who joined us for dinner after the other doctors left, ate everything, and in large quantities. We were afraid of the water and stuck to bottled drinks. Ali assured us that the water was perfectly safe. It turned out he was right. The purifying plant the British had installed turned the brown lethal brew of the Tigris into clear, safe, and palatable water. But we needed lots of reassuring from other quarters before *we* felt safe in drinking it.

Building the Basics

Joan

EARLY EACH MORNING, while we stayed at the Semiramis Hotel, a taxi shrieked to a halt in front and blasted its arrival. Diesel fumes enveloped it momentarily. "*Sahib!* Doctor Baez!" the driver announced, as he stood, a shabby sentinel, by his open door. This was the third week that Al had gone house-hunting.

"If they'd only put street names somewhere, or numbers," he said, bumping the sides of his head with his open palms. There were no maps or help from the local Unesco office. Al was at the mercy of the goodnatured taxi driver, whose mind was more on his meter than on new housing for this American.

Sometimes when Pauline went house-hunting with Al, she gave me graphic descriptions of what our future home might be like. The kitchen was always the most important. "They're all caves, Mum. Spooky. You can't see when you go in. The windows are small and covered with yards of burlap that hang on a rod and swing back and forth all day because some little boy keeps it wet by throwing pails of water over them and swings them and that's supposed to keep everything cool." I didn't like the hopeless tone in her voice.

"Most of the kitchens have dirt floors and the servants squat on them to do all their work, usually by candlelight," she said.

"They have big metal dishpans they use to wash their rice or clean the spinach. One of those women was squatting in a bunch of mud, washing her clothes. I saw the mud squishing up between her toes and the water was the same color. Ick!"

"No running water at all? No sink?" I asked, genuinely interested. "What do they cook on?"

"Well," she said, "they have funny little braziers or sometimes a kerosene burner right on the floor and they cook the whole meal on it. It's so hot and smelly and they always have a cigarette dangling from their mouths. It really is yicky."

I felt a victim already.

Our hopes waned; Al looked haggard and discouraged.

Then one day salvation walked in the door: our friend, Ali Kamal, showed up with his wife and two little girls about Mimi's age. He was a great tall Arab from Palestine with a rumpled haystack of reddish brown hair, a nose that covered a third of his face, and a bristling mustache and he was dressed in a brown business suit that hung loose and wrinkled over his thin body. He spoke beautiful English and he radiated an air of self-confidence that comforted Al and me.

Ali's wife, Jeanne, who was two months pregnant, had just arrived from England, where Ali had received his degree in medicine. He would now work at the Baghdad hospital. Jeanne would do what I would do, be a good housewife and mother.

I liked Jeanne immediately. She was so British, her voice was quiet and gentle. She leaned slightly forward when she walked, as caring people often do, in a kind of ready-to-help posture. Jeanne was a brave lady, too. She had weathered the horror of having seen her first husband as a young soldier burned to death in an airplane crash while she waited at the airport on his return from the war. A couple of years later she married Ali, who had told her of his dreams of going to America to live. He wanted to take her with him. She looked forward to that more than any other dream she had. Now, however, she was trying, as I was trying, to find the things about this strange land that we could enjoy and respect.

The day that Ali Kamal walked into the hotel lobby and

found us drooping with discouragement, he strode over to Al and said, "You have been hunting for a house. So have I. It is very difficult. Tomorrow, we shall go together to the North Gate, and we shall find a house. You must believe that." Al was dubious, but he thanked Ali for his offer.

They were off early in the morning. Ali found a brand-new, not quite completed, large house. It was being built for a nursing home, but as at the moment there were no doctors or nurses to staff it, Ali talked to the owner about our two families renting it together. It was at the North Gate, just outside the city of Baghdad in a section of town called Al Waziria. The two men took little time deciding that we could live together. I was delighted. There were their two children, Susan and Gay-Gay, ages about two and four, playmates for Mimi. I would have somebody to talk to. There were no tourists or foreigners here, so perhaps the other two girls would find some Iraqi children for friends.

Al had one concern about living together. Ali was Moslem and we were Quakers. Would our different customs possibly make tensions between the two families? But Ali had no qualms when Al spoke to him about it. "My good friend," Ali said, "I don't suppose you're any more of a practicing Quaker than I am a practicing Moslem." He smiled, having no idea that Al was a very active Quaker. The question of renting the house together was settled.

Mud huts and empty fields surrounded the tall iron gate and taller cement wall with its familiar jagged glass spikes on top to help deter thieves. A dirt road wound its way past our house and a few others, becoming scantier as it wound away from the village. Some Army soldiers and colonels, middle-class merchants, and store owners lived there. The mud huts were rented by poor and unloved families who worked the fields, when the season was right, to produce vegetables—beets, spinach, lettuce—for the meager living, the pittance, their wealthy landlords gave them.

Inside the gate of the house was an ant hill of activity. About twenty men and a half dozen little boys wearing only loin-clothes or Baghdad jodhpurs (long skirts that pull up from the back between the legs and tuck tightly around the waist), heaved buckets of cement, bricks and pails of water, one to the other, down a long work line to where the building was going on at the moment. The boys carried gravel and stones in pails and baskets on their heads. They looked awkward, but they managed to balance them with little trouble. Sweat poured in rivulets down the muscled backs and legs of the workmen, but they moved on like slow-motion machines. Now and then a little boy stopped, grinned, showing his sturdy white teeth. "*Saba, saba, Memsah*," he called, then marched on.

They all walked barefoot on the rocks, the gravel, and the dry, caked mud baked by the scorching sun. Commanding and directing the crew was ageless Mahal, who looked to me like a walking bronze statue. He was a slight man. His skin was stretched over his bones and muscles like thin brown paint. He smiled often, I think to show us his two gold front teeth. His one good eye was bloodshot always and we never found out if he had any hair because he never removed his ragged black and white turban.

Somebody had given Mahal an Army trench coat. It must have been long, long ago, for the buttons and belt were gone and it was starched well with cement and paint. It hung over his skimpy body like a pup tent. I'm sure shoes had never caressed his feet.

We called Mahal our gate-keeper, but that was the least of his jobs. He recruited his bewildered men and boys, worked with them from 6 A.M. till noon, digging, cementing, painting, plumbing, wiring for electric light, hauling and dumping building materials. Everything looked so heavy. At noon the men and boys dropped work, found a spot of shade, ate their sammoun, drank their tea, smoked, chatted, and slept until 4, when the ant hill became active again.

While we were moving in, the men were still cementing in windows, hanging doors, placing and gluing in floor tiles, always with a brown-stained damp quarter-inch of a cigarette dangling from their lips. When they finished they simply spat the butt on the floor, making one more brown stain on the blue-gray cement. The smell of stale Turkish tobacco and damp cement permeated the whole area.

Mahal slept on our front porch. He unrolled a straw mat and there he curled up in his Army coat. I think most of the night he wandered over the grounds listening for a click of the gate or the crackle of a tree branch just beyond it.

At last the tall-ceilinged stone twenty-by-forty-square-foot living room, the four downstairs bedrooms, and the hall were finished. The cement outdoor stairs led to our family's quarters, where there were another four bedrooms, ready for beds and bodies to inhabit.

Mahal said when the workmen finished inserting the copper-cement fireguard over the three-burner kerosene stove in the kitchen we women could go in and take action.

We were excited to get in. But oh—it looked bare and impractical, in fact, downright depressing to this comfort-loving Californian. No table space or sinkboard, no hot water or ventilation, and only one faucet over the dwarf sink. Ah, but we had a 25-watt light bulb dangling naked from the center of the ceiling and there were the blue and white squares of tile over the sink to gaze at while we waited for the water to gurgle down the skinny drain. Why was I griping?

"Will we have a bathroom, Ali?" I asked, picturing some weird outdoor arrangement with no privacy or drainage.

"My dear, you will have your Western bathroom and there will be two Eastern ones," he said, like a father to a spoiled child. Ali was a sexist to his very bones, and truly, I was no more than a child in his eyes. Fortunately for me, Jeanne too hoped for the civilized touch and Ali said that we must all share the one big Western bathroom. They would have their private Eastern one and we ours.

Luxury, I thought. There were few modern bathrooms even in the rich quarters, and there were fewer workmen who had seen one. The old Eastern type consisted of a hole in the floor with a container that was emptied by a servant into a nearby bin or gutter. The odor was numbing. There was also the new

Eastern-type with a flush porcelain bowl deep in the floor. We were introduced to those at the Semiramis Hotel and we learned to stand clear of the splash when we pulled the chain. The workmen would even mold footprints to position the customer correctly.

Under the shade of the porch roof, even before we were completely moved in, Jeanne and I discovered our permanent "porchperch" overlooking the huge mud patch that was our backyard. There we watched the men at work, sometimes squatting on their heels in the dust, chatting, laughing, drawing pictures in the dirt, pictures, we hoped, of plans for our Western bathroom's pipelines and connections.

It took three weeks of plotting, hauling, laying in the pipes, and placing the bathroom equipment on the cement floor. We watched Mahal and his workers sweat and groan while carrying in an old V-shaped bathtub. Mahal attached a wide cloth strap around his forehead and another around his waist, then he pulled while his men lifted the back end of the tub and pushed at each step that Mahal took. The tub would serve only skinny folk, we learned later. In fact, even those of us with little flesh had to lie on one hip and splash the water over the rest of the body. The obese could only roll.

An Italian bidet was next, the kind that many Americans mistake for a urinal when they meet one in Italy or France. Then came a porcelain sink for running water and the "pièce de résistance," last and best, a real flush sit-down toilet with a box overhead that read *"The Great Niagra,"* spelled just like that.

Late one afternoon, Mahal, dressed in his Army trench coat, his face and hands cleansed of plaster and paint, his gold teeth gleaming, and his mud-spattered feet stepping more lightly than usual, came toward me. "Memsah, memsah," he beckoned. There stood all his workers in the doorway of his most important production—our western bathroom. The men dipped their heads graciously. Their focus shone as brightly as the bathroom copper and brass attachments. A pipe jutted out from one wall—for the shower, I figured. There was even a drain in the center of the floor. Emergencies, I suspected. Of course, there was the finishing touch of blue and white tile behind the sink.

"Oh Mahal!" I exclaimed. If he had known our Western ways, I would have hugged him with all his grime and sweat. But what they really would like, I knew, were some extra *dinars*. I motioned them all to wait right there while I ran in for my purse. Not a bare foot had budged when I returned. They took the dinars with respectful silence and a bow, each in turn, then they were off chattering, laughing, and lighting up their cigarettes.

While the men continued to work on our new house, we moved in slowly. Sometimes I stood on our fenced-in roof, looking at the scene around us. I wouldn't forget this picturesque neighborhood, so totally different from ours at home. On one side was a long, low view of the city of Baghdad, its minarets and mosques jutting into a low and level skyline, the squat houses nearby where women in their black abayahs moved slowly in and out the doors with pails and bundles and babies. Near us were the mud huts. In front of them in the mornings the women did most of their chores. They spread newspaper or old cloth, even a small carpet if they boasted any money at all, placed their hibachi stove beside it or built a small fire with sticks. Most of the women spent at least the mornings on that spot, where they cooked, nursed babies, fed their families, and gossiped with their neighboring female friends. The small boys in their long dresses played with their young friends, always boys, or left with their fathers to work at the zucs, selling British cloth at the fabric booth, or at the copper market beating out bowls, or maybe on construction jobs such as our house. After the age of seven, a boy's place was with his father and he was to be respected.

Not so the little girls. They had a harder lot. I could see them out in the field collecting cow-chips and sticks for the fires, mounting bundles on their heads so huge that their faces became invisible. They tended their small brothers and sisters, and helped with the clotheswashing, which they did in metal basins on the ground. They accompanied their mothers to the markets and when they got their meager supply of food, the little girls helped cook it. They were born to be servants, to work. As far as I saw, they knew nothing of dolls and dress-ups or even playing together.

I liked the road view in front best. There I could watch the vendors with baskets of oranges or sammoun on their heads, see the old men herd their donkeys with huge panniers of sticks and straw down the dusty road. Sometimes little boys rode on their backs. Occasionally, a camel strode proudly by, his owner always beside him. The camel, too, was weighted on both sides with panniers. How could he walk with such dignity with that funny-looking face, I wondered.

Up there, I was above the dwarf eucalyptus trees that were dust-laden from spring to winter when the rains washed them. If I looked straight down, there was our garbage pail usually alive with cats and sometimes children—rummaging around in it to find bits of whatever we had left from the night before.

I could see Old Pudding, the Captain across the street, whom we got to know later, sitting on his threadbare easy chair on the porch, smoking his hubble-bubble pipe. Above me in the early mornings and evenings the sky turned to a pink-golden color. It always made me think of the song "Jerusalem the Golden," hardly appropriate. I liked that quiet spot, kind of a compensation for the hubbub and rattle of the world below.

About a month after we were somewhat settled in and the bathroom was pronounced ready for use, Pauline and I decided to put it to the test. In those sweltering days, a cold shower could be termed only the height of luxury, and we had it! Pauline said, with a little uncertainty in her voice, "I think I'll take a shower."

"Wonderful idea," I returned. "Why don't I try out the sink with real running water? Just think, I can get rid of our quaint archaic pitcher and bowl device."

She, in her tidy way, folded her clothes and put them on the floor in a corner away from the waterworks. I turned to the sink, fully dressed, to wash my face, when Pauline announced, "Here we go, Mom. Baghdad special!" On came the water full force like a fireman's hose. A walloping splat, then the uncontrolled jet rushed to every wall and bounced back. I grabbed the clothes, Pauline leapt for the faucets, and I left her in the rising lake. The magnificent drain in the center was too clogged with plaster and paint to swallow the water. When I returned with a dry towel, Pauline was squatting by the drain picking and digging out the cement with comb and toothbrush, convulsed with laughter. We watched rivulets winding down the hall, into the bedroom, the kitchen, and under our cushions on the porch. I straddled some of the streams and handed her a dry towel.

"So much for the Baghdad special, Mom!" she called, as she ran out of the bathroom, hair dripping down her back.

I thought as I pushed the muddy water down the wonder drain with my burlap-rag mop, down you go, trouble. We'll just go on building the basics.

Al Waziria

Al

WE LIVED IN THE old part of Baghdad at the northern end of town called Al Waziria, where the ministries of foreign countries were situated ("wazir" means "minister"). It was near the road which leads to the old mosque at Khadhimain. From Al Waziria, looking across the Tigris, you could see groves of date palms and old homes in the distance.

We lived in a neighborhood of sharp contrasts. Some of the legation buildings were of modern construction and painted white, but most of them were old mud-colored structures. All of them were large, and some of them were elegant. Yet up the street from our modern white house, people lived in huts made completely of mud except for the palmleaf roof. As we walked by them we could see women making cow dung patties and setting them out to dry to be used as fuel for cooking. This kind of work was done by women and girls. The men and the boys never touched the cow dung. There was a shortage of fuel so women and children spent hours collecting twigs and scraps of anything that could be burned, recycled, or sold. Some little children were carrying bundles larger than themselves.

Within three blocks of our home we could reach the legations of Pakistan, India, and the USSR, as well as the British cultural center, called the British Institute, where Iraqis could read

English books and magazines. All of these buildings had their respective flags flying high. Within their courtyards we could see people dressed in the typical costumes of their countries. I liked in particular the tight white trousers and the coats with high collars worn by the men from Pakistan. It was a welcome relief to see Indian women dressed in pink and blue saris rather than in the monotonous black abayah universally worn by Bahgdadi women. In contrast, some wealthy Iraqi men wore elegant tan or dark brown robes embroidered with gold.

Seeing real poverty for the first time at such close range made a lasting impression on all of us—especially on our children. In California we had lived in a typical middle-class house in a college town, where we did not see extremes of wealth or poverty. In Baghdad, on the other hand, we were living in a neighborhood where people of affluence and influence lived right next to people living in mud huts. We noticed that children from the poor mud huts came and took food which we had discarded and had put out for the garbage man to collect. Joan dreaded doing this because a swarm of cats would leap all over her when she came out of the house.

"Look," said Joan one day, "the children are eating the rotten pomegranates I threw out this morning."

She was distressed by this contrast between our life style and theirs and one day tried to give the children some oranges. The children ran away when she approached them. They were not used to having anyone give them anything. Joan then started the practice of putting bread and other bits of food in a bundle which the children could reach by climbing but which the ever-present dogs and cats could not reach. If she put this food out at night it was gone by the crack of dawn.

The problems Joan faced in feeding and keeping us healthy were no less daunting for her than those I faced in my Unesco mission. The shift from supermarket shopping in California to item-by-item shopping in the zucs and bazaars, facing the hurdles of differences in weights, language, and money was as intimidating for her as confronting the Dean of the college was for me.

Fortunately, Ali's wife, Jeanne, was very friendly and helpful. Joan and Jeanne were able to share the single kitchen and its kerosene stove without incident for two reasons: the Baezes and the Kamals worked on very different time schedules, and Jeanne and Joan were both sensitive and accommodating.

"How are you and Jeanne doing in the kitchen?" I asked.

"Just fine. Jeanne is very unobtrusive and friendly and I try to be the same."

The two women had agreed it would be better if neither one tried to cook meals for both families.

Jeanne said, "You know, Joan, Ali is very fond of fried meat for breakfast. I've noticed that you concentrate on fruit and cereals instead. Ali loves fried kidneys, liver, and brains." And then, with a grimace, "Can you imagine? The brains look like so many little mice in the frying pan! And they have to be cooked in goat grease!"

We couldn't *stand* the smell of the goat grease! It permeated the whole house. If you happened not to feel well there was nothing that could make you feel worse!

In time, as Joan and Jeanne got to know each other, they would have liked to be together in the kitchen just for company, but they made it a point to stay out of each other's way, and it worked.

Our diet was much simpler than theirs partly because we had difficulty in obtaining the things we were used to and did without them. Life became smoother—but not less expensive—when Joan discovered Spinney's, a British-owned store where the attendants, mostly Syrian, spoke English. And they delivered your purchases to your home. There Joan felt safe to buy lamb, which was plentiful, and chickens, which were occasionally available. We discovered packaged date cubes with almonds, and they became a staple of our diet along with bananas—safe because they could be peeled—and tomatoes, which we also peeled. We were wary of leafy vegetables and washed them in sodium permanganate. Pistachio nuts were so plentiful and cheap that we munched on them continuously. At Spinney's we found British corn flakes, but milk was a problem.

We had brought some powdered milk with us, but in those days powdered milk was not easily soluble. Eventually we found a woman who could bring her buffalo into the front yard. She wore the usual black abayah. She asked us for a funnel and a bottle, squatted down and milked the buffalo in front of us—a charmed audience—squirting the white fluid deftly into the funnel. Of course it had to be boiled.

What About Milk, Ali?

Joan

"WHAT ABOUT MILK, ALI?" I asked one day.

"My dear, you will drink only powdered milk. Never buy fresh milk until I tell you it's all right." He looked concerned. "I am going to ask at a clean dairy with pasteurization. Until then, you will buy the Golden Crown powdered brand and be safe."

We had already tried it. We had mixed boiled water with the yellowish powder, squashed the doughy lumps and stirred thoroughly. Result, a gluey liquid and a taste like Milk of Magnesia. We tried pouring in treacle, canned chocolate from Spinney's store, powdered coffee. Still the brand name of Elmer's glue came up in the conversation every time we tried to drink it.

I understood Ali's warning when the girls and I went for a walk down an alley behind some houses one morning. We heard a weak kind of a "muuu" and turned to see behind us an emaciated cow with a rope around her neck being led by an old woman. Bones protruded in lines around the cow's rib cage like a washboard and her poor old knuckles stood up wherever she was jointed. Her milk bag sagged and her head drooped.

"Here comes the dairy, Mom," Pauline chirped. She always had a way of making me laugh.

The woman stopped at the back of a nearby house and

banged on it with the palm of her hand. She shouted something that we guessed was "Milk!" The door opened and a little girl handed the dairy-woman two empty Coke bottles. The cow stood still and the woman took out a funnel from somewhere under her long black dress. Then she squatted down to the bag that was covered with flies, as were her hands. She began to squeeze and pull those wrinkled teats until a fine stream of blue milk jutted out in a straight line into the funnel. Somehow the poor old beast managed to fill both bottles.

She handed the bottles back to the child who had been silently watching. They exchanged some money, bowed farewell, and the old woman thumped her bare feet on down the dusty road leading her wretched cow.

"Poor old things," Joanie said, looking thoughtful. She searched in her pockets. "I don't even have a candy to give her."

For the next few moments we walked on silently. The whole world centered on the old woman and her cow. Was there anything but hunger and sadness anywhere?

Just then, by the gutter, we saw about a dozen little boys in long red flannel dresses playing jacks with stones. They all looked up and grinned. I saw Joanie bat her eyes at them, and she called, "*Salaam alekum* (hello)!" They giggled, put up their hands hesitantly, looked down and up again, then answered, "Sabah, sabah."

Hmmm, I thought, kids playing marbles with no marbles, no shoes, no lunch, no milk for sure, no nothing. But they laughed, flirted, played. Look at them, I thought. Are they telling me something? Yes, something definite.

We wandered on home and when Ali came home, I called to him, "Ali, forget the milk. The Yellow Crown will do."

"But my goodness, is this true?" he teased. "My question is, will you survive?"

"Just possibly," I laughed back.

University College

Al

HAVING OVERCOME OUR first hurdle—housing—I could begin to concentrate on the Unesco mission that had brought me to Baghdad: assisting the University College, with the aid of my team, to begin establishing departments of physics, chemistry, and biology by teaching courses in these subjects.

When I left the house in the morning I simply forgot, for the time being, the enormous problems Joan had to contend with. These included finding schools for the girls and keeping all of us well fed and healthy.

I usually took a bus from a stop near our house in Al Waziria, although occasionally I walked; either way, it took about 30 minutes. The bus left me at the North Gate, Bab El Muatham, at the intersection of Rashid and Ghazi streets. It was the noisiest street corner in the world. Every conceivable mode of ground transportation, with the exception of trains, used it as a terminal. The most colorful were the horse-drawn carriages, called *arabanas*. They were rickety and their wheels wobbled. Their horses were thin and ill-fed and they were treated cruelly. In England these four-wheeled phaetons, with no side pieces in front of the seat, had been an elegant conveyance. But in Bab El Muatham you sometimes saw them loaded with dead sheep being taken to the marketplace along the dirt road called Ghazi Street, parallel to Rashid but bending here to intersect with it.

The red double-decker buses from England used this corner as a terminal, and so did the small cheaper buses that brought people from afar to the marketplaces of Baghdad. On these some of the passengers rode on the roof, weighting down their baggage so it wouldn't fly off.

Right near this noisy and smelly center of human activity and confusion were two of Baghdad's colleges. One was the Queen Alliah College for women. The other, across a wide street was the one in which the Unesco team worked. It was variously called the University College, emulating the British institution; the University of Baghdad, of which it considered itself as the nucleus; or the College of Arts and Sciences, which was probably the closest interpretation of *Kuliet de Ledab wa Lalum*, as it was called in Arabic.

I wish I could say that the brick wall surrounding the college enclosed a quiet green campus like that of Oxford or Cambridge. But such was not the case. No lawns. No ivy. Just one decrepit brown building in a state of disrepair.

It was, nevertheless, a symbol of change. One obvious proof of this was that all women students who, outside the wall, wore the black abayah covering them from head to foot, removed it as soon as they passed the entrance gate. They wore western-style dresses beneath the abayah and interacted socially with the men students in a natural and unselfconscious way. This was more than I could say for the wife of the Dean, who remained in her kitchen when we visited them on a later occasion.

Everyone spoke Arabic, naturally, except those of us who came from other countries. We spoke English regardless of our country of origin. Someone has said, jokingly mixing metaphors, that broken English is the lingua franca of the modern world, but all the Arabic members of the college faculty spoke perfect Oxford English.

This was particularly true of the Dean of the college, who spoke with a pronounced British accent. He also smoked English tobacco in a pipe which he fussed with continuously.

Dean Duri was a short, energetic and nervous man with a shining bald head and dark eyes that flashed with intensity and humor most of the time—although I did see him explode with annoyance and anger on a few occasions. His favorite expression when he conversed with me was, "Right you are, Professor Baez, right you are!"

"You know, Dean Duri," I said in one of our early meetings, "I need the answers to a lot of questions before I can settle down to teaching. For example: Where are my students? How can I find them? Or, how can they find me? What courses am I supposed to teach? What classrooms should I use? Is there a physics laboratory, and if so, where is it? Where can I obtain textbooks to teach from?"

"Right you are, Professor Baez, right you are. I will find someone to help you in getting answers to all of these questions."

But it was clear that I had overwhelmed him with too many questions at one time. If I had understood Arabic I would have found the answers for myself. He was just not prepared to deal with an international team coming in ignorant of their language and customs.

I had been given a fourfold assignment: to coordinate the activities of the Unesco team, to start research work in some relevant field, to organize laboratory work, and to teach the physics courses. Before I could teach I had to find my students.

As a result of a series of coincidences and accidents—which is the way *everything* happened in Baghdad, it seemed—I found them. I must have been looking lost and bewildered standing in the corridor one day, when a good-looking, well-dressed, olive-skinned and green-eyed young man with slightly curly hair introduced himself. "I am Hassan Ahmed Hassan. Are you, by any chance, Professor Baez?"

"Yes, I am. How did you know?"

"I just guessed. You are obviously a stranger. I am a student in your third year optics class."

"Wonderful! I have been looking for my students but I didn't know where to find them."

"The information is posted on the bulletin board. Come with me and I'll show you." We walked together down the corridor full of students. He pointed to the board. Everything was in Arabic. I couldn't understand a word. My facial expression told Hassan the story. He understood and he blushed. This is something I will always remember about Hassan: he blushed at the slightest provocation. He obviously empathized with me and seemed to feel guilty for not having taken my ignorance of his language into account. He wrote down a complete English translation of everything that was relevant to me.

Hassan was a Palestinian. He became my volunteer assistant in all academic matters. He turned out to be my most brilliant student as well. He took me to the room where my first-year students had been waiting for me. They had been doing this for several days, waiting for a while and then leaving when I did not arrive. Hassan called the stragglers in from the corridors and introduced me. He stayed long enough to see that things got started and then left me alone with the class.

I had both men and women in my first year class. They were all well dressed—conservatively, nothing extravagant or elegant—in western-style clothes. They were obviously members of the upper middle class. They were noisy and almost childlike in their behavior in a group situation but very friendly and polite when confronted individually.

We started meeting on a regular basis in a classroom in which the only visual aid was a coarse chalkboard that chewed up the soft chalk sticks so that I was left covered with chalk dust at the end of every lecture. I missed not having physics demonstration apparatus. I had to resort to improvisation with simple things like a key tied to a string for a pendulum. Even the simplest things described in the Unesco *Sourcebook for Science Teaching* would have come in handy, but this and all my other books were still in a trunk at the airport even several weeks after our arrival. We measured the period of the simple pendulum with my wristwatch. I linked rubber bands to illustrate the properties of springs. I brought my tape recorder into the class—a complete novelty in those days and a tremendous hit. We demonstrated the properties of sound, varying the pitch of the sounds of music and speech by running it at different speeds and listening, with amusement, to a tape run backwards. It was clear that this kind of behavior in a classroom was something novel for them. Word got around that physics, demonstrated experimentally, was understandable and enjoyable. But the opportunity for students to do hands-on experiments by themselves was missing. I resolved to remedy that.

Everything took time. No matter how simple it was it took time to resolve. Like finding textbooks for my classes. It was up to me to decide what to do about textbooks. There was only one store in Baghdad—Mackenzie's—that carried science textbooks in English. They had no physics texts at all when I visited. I was told they had to be ordered from England. They were expensive and would take at least six weeks to arrive. The clerk said they would gladly have ordered them earlier if they had known what books we wanted and how many copies would be needed. They should, of course, have been ordered the previous semester.

Once again, this problem was solved through a series of coincidences. I was, by chance, visiting the Baghdad office of the United States Information Service (USIS). They were glad to see a fellow American in Baghdad and offered to help me. Also by chance they had twenty copies of an American physics text, Haussman and Slack, which had been printed as paperbacks for the U.S. Army. By sharing these, my first year students had access to a physics text that year.

Once the semester got rolling it was not possible to speak to the Dean in private. Too many other members of the staff wanted his attention as well, so the custom was for the Dean to sit at a desk on a raised platform in a large and empty classroom whose walls were lined with chairs for visitors who wished to speak with him. It was a democratic approach. In principle anyone could have access to the Dean this way. No one was excluded. But the associated formalities made it difficult to get even one question answered.

The ritual went something like this: the *farash* who stood

guard at the door as you approached gave you a military-style salute, lacking, however, the crisp motions of the real thing. Instead of a uniform he wore a rather ragged and ill-fitting shirt and trousers. Besides, he was friendly and smiled at you—not at all what you would expect from the guards at Buckingham Palace.

The farash would let you into the large room and there would be Dean Duri at his desk at the far end of the room. There would, typically, be three or four other faculty members already there sitting rather formally in their chairs. Dean Duri would look up from the pile of papers in front of him and acknowledge you with a nod as you took your seat.

"Good morning, Professor Baez." He *always* called me Professor. "Will you have some tea?"

I nodded, but even before I had done so Dean Duri had pressed a button at the end of a long wire and you could hear a loud electric bell like a fire gong ringing at the end of the outside corridor. The farash entered, looking somewhat dazed, awaiting instructions. Dean Duri would shout at him *"Gib chai!"* one of the first expressions I learned in Arabic, meaning "bring tea."

I nodded at the others who had come in ahead of me. We didn't speak to one another. They nodded back politely. You could tell the order in which they had entered the room by noting the stage at which their tea drinking had progressed.

I was very reluctant to drink anything that might make me sick, but I figured the tea was safe since it had been boiled. I was more worried about germs on the glass in which the tea was served. But I knew my interview with the Dean would never get started until he saw that I had had my tea.

I had by now discovered that drinking tea was an obligatory routine before discussing matters of substance with anyone. During my first few weeks in Baghdad, when I had to visit so many new people to get my questions answered, I often had to go through the tea ceremony as many as eight or ten times in one day.

The tea was strong and very sweet. It was served in a little torso-shaped glass on a saucer. In order to avoid sugar shock from an excess of glucose and in order to minimize the risk of contagion, I developed a technique that enabled me to disinfect the top edge of the glass—or so I hoped—and not have to drink too much tea.

I would stir my tea vigorously with the tiny spoon that came with it, making sure that the hot tea washed the upper edge of the glass. In the process I also made sure that about half the contents spilled out over the edge and into the saucer. I would smile vacuously at my colleagues while I stirred my tea in order to divert their attention from my glass-washing procedure. Since the tea glass was only about half-full to begin with, by sloshing half of what was left into the saucer I was left with about a quarter of a glass of tea. I now waited until the Dean was looking straight at me and put the glass to my lips, holding the glass there but only taking an occasional sip. I thus fulfilled my social obligation and ensured that the Dean was aware of it.

Suddenly the Dean would indicate by a nod that it was my turn to speak. I had a list of about six questions, but by now there were about five new faculty members in the room and I was under great pressure to be brief.

"Dean Duri," I said, "I need to have a complete list of all the students in my classes."

"Right you are, Professor Baez," said Duri as he rang for Mulahed, who was the secretary of the College. When Mulahed appeared Duri explained to him in explosive Arabic what I presumed was the essence of my request, motioning me to follow Mulahed to his office.

Thus, after waiting for about twenty minutes I had gotten the answer to only one of my six questions. I would have to come back many more times and repeat the tea ceremony each time. In the meantime, new questions would arise. It was clear that I had to find a new solution to my communication problem.

If I had a phone, I thought, I would have direct access to the Dean without the complication of the tea ritual. Once, when I had visited the Dean in his office, I noticed that he dropped whatever he was doing when the phone rang and concentrated on answering the phone personally, giving it the highest priority.

I was determined to get a phone installed in my office. I pulled all the strings I could think of, including my rank as chief of the Unesco mission. I told Duri that he owed it to Unesco to give us all possible assistance. I also had the valid excuse that the proposed new physics lab was going to be in a building three blocks away from my office. A phone was absolutely necessary to communicate with my assistants there.

I had been told that it was a forlorn hope to expect to get a phone in less than two months. Others had waited as long as six months. But I pleaded my case almost daily with the Dean, and in about a week a telephone had been installed in my office, which also served as Unesco headquarters. Never before in the history of Baghdad, I was told, had anyone ever obtained a telephone as quickly as that.

But now I could cut the time of an appointment with the Dean from twenty minutes down to about three. I was always very courteous on the phone. I took my time to get to the point. Without having to go through the tea ceremony I could afford to seem leisurely and indulge in some pleasantries. I had learned to say "good morning" in Arabic.

"*SabaH el khair*, Doctor Duri."

"Right you are, Professor Baez," he said with a chuckle. "I see you have learned Arabic!"

Naseeb Dajani

Al

AS MY WORK LOAD increased I felt the need for a combination interpreter, typist, and messenger boy.

I said to Dean Duri, "Unesco has set aside ten dinars per month to pay for such a helper."

"Right you are, Professor Baez, right you are. But you know this presents difficulties for me. We have to create a post and it will have to be filled on the basis of competitive examinations. It will take time."

Coming from a free-wheeling California background, I felt there must be some way of circumventing the rules in our case. Unesco had sent the money directly to me. I felt I should be able to hire someone on the open market without having to create a special post. I went ahead on that assumption and began recruiting by word of mouth.

One day a young man came to my office to apply for the job. He was tall, good looking, athletic, and obviously intelligent. His name was Naseeb Dajani. He had the dark skin characteristic of this part of the world.

"I hear you have an opening for an assistant," he said.

"Who told you about it?"

"Mr. Roberts at the office of the American attaché. He told me you are American."

"That's true, but I'm here as an international civil servant. I need an energetic young person to help me with various tasks. You speak Arabic, of course?"

"Yes, I also speak French. I am a Palestinian. My family fled from our homeland when the Jews moved into Palestine." He pronounced it "Palesteen."

I was impressed with Naseeb's aristocratic demeanor, his tact, and his deference. He had a cultured voice. He spoke with a British accent. He was a gentleman. It was clear he could be an effective messenger and interpreter. But I also needed a typist. That was a lot to ask for ten dinars a month.

"Can you type?" I asked.

His smile gave me the answer: that he was not the world's best typist but that he could certainly learn quickly if this was a job requirement. The way he fumbled as he fed the paper into the typewriter suggested that his experience had probably been limited to pecking away at a few term papers. He was, nevertheless, an impressive young man. I was convinced that he could pick up this skill on his own.

"How old are you?"

Naseeb blushed imperceptibly. "Nineteen," he said after a short pause and a gulp. He looked older. I went to Dean Duri and told him I wanted to hire Naseeb.

The Dean said this was impossible and gave technical reasons for it. Basically, however, it was because he was under pressure to give jobs to Iraqis and not to Palestinians. This was a delicate point. Many of the Palestinian refugees were, it seemed to me, more highly qualified and more energetic then the average Iraqi. I didn't want to make invidious comparisons, but when I became convinced that Naseeb was my man I pushed for hiring him with a tenacity that surprised the Dean. By this time Dean Duri had seen that I was completely dedicated to my work, that I worked longer hours than most of the other faculty members and made do with inadequate classrooms and labs. In short, he sensed I had come to work. . . . So, before long, Dean Duri acceded to my demand and I hired Naseeb. We never regretted it. Of all the people I met that year in Baghdad, Naseeb is the only one who became a life-long personal friend. He eventually followed me to California, graduated from Stanford, and went on to work for Unesco. Thirty years after Baghdad, Naseeb and I collaborated on humanitarian and conservation projects. Only then did he confess that when he applied for the post in Baghdad he was only fifteen, not nineteen! He had never in his life typed before that. He had borrowed a typewriter and practiced every night for the first two weeks.

With Naseeb and a telephone to help me I felt I could solve any problem that came my way in Baghdad. I would have plenty of opportunities to prove it.

As the weeks rolled on, taking the bus to the college every morning became routine. Normally, after you sat in your seat on the bus, the conductor would step up to you to sell you a ticket. One morning, however, as I was about to give the conductor my 14 *fils* he refused to take my money. To explain, he pointed to the rear of the bus where I saw Mulahed, the executive secretary of the college. He had paid my fare. I nodded thanks. He nodded back and so did several students who were with him. It was a custom in Baghdad to vie for first place in buying tickets for all your friends on the bus.

Mulahed did this on several other occasions. I would always nod thanks and he would acknowledge me with a nod, a bow, and a smile. I wanted to repay him in some way for this courtesy, so one day I walked back a few blocks and boarded the bus one stop before Mulahed's. That day as he boarded the bus with some students, I beckoned the conductor and quickly bought tickets for all of them. They hadn't noticed that I was on the bus.

When the conductor approached them they were about to pay for their own tickets and for mine but the conductor pointed in my direction and told them I had already paid. Now it was my turn to look back and return their thanks with a nod, a low and exaggeratedly gracious bow, and a smile. They were taken by surprise and overcome with mirth. Mulahed never got over that incident. He enjoyed telling the story over and over again to the Dean and to anyone who would listen.

Naseeb, Our Happy Accident

Joan

ABOUT A MONTH after we were settled and Al had a spot for his work, a happy accident happened one day when a tall and handsome Palestinian Arab named Naseeb Dajani walked into Al's office at the university. He was young, bright, and moved unbelievably quickly for someone in that part of the world. Best of all, he was anxious to work. He greeted Al with a wide smile that showed strong white teeth and he said, "You are Dr. Baez, are you not? And you are looking for a secretary, izzent-it? I am a bery good secretary. My name is Naseeb Dajani. I am from Palestine. Perhaps I will work for you?"

Al liked his honest face and the look of intelligence in his eyes. His English was excellent. "Can you type?" Al asked the tall Arab.

"Yes, Sair, of course, bedy well indeed, Sair."

"Can you type a good business letter?" Al went on.

"Yes, Sair, I type it bedy well." A few more questions and Al gave him the morning's letters to sort and type, feeling relieved that at last here was some efficient help. Naseeb smiled graciously, took the letters, and began to sort.

He told us many years later that he was perspiring when he left the office, and he worked on the typewriter all night, "until my eyes were making it double everything. Oh, I suffer very

48

much because I did not learn fast enough. I wanted to work with this great American physicist."

Al knew by the salutation on the first letter that Naseeb was not 'a bedy good typist,' not even a good one, but he liked this nineteen-year-old boy. He'd probably learn quickly and Al would help him. He was impressed with Naseeb's enthusiasm.

The first time he came to dinner, I liked his polite, positive manner. The kids said he knew how to talk to them. We all welcomed his easy laugh and I could see that this happy accident would be more than a secretary to Al. For that, I was glad.

After Naseeb had worked for some weeks, we sat at tea in our patio one day and Naseeb said, "Dr. Baez, Sair, do you ever like to take a day away from work, Sair?"

Al folded his arms over his chest, winked at me because that was a question from all of us that seldom had a positive answer. "Well, I would like to, but you see all there is to be done and there's no time."

"Yes, Sair," Naseeb returned, ignoring Al's excuses. "What about this Friday, our religious day off? This week you will be a Moslem and have a free day. We can take the family to Ctesiphon. This is a beautiful stone arch, five hundred feet high, the ruins of a palace of the third century, A.D. It is not too many miles away and my family lives on the way. We can stop and rest there. My mother and six sisters, my brother and beautiful Zuzu, who is my nephew, will like it bedy much to see you, all of you."

The girls' faces brightened up as they glanced one to the other, then to me. Al could see that whether he liked it or not, we would go to Ctesiphon.

It sounded exciting. We wondered, imagined, planned in anticipation until Friday arrived with Naseeb in a rattling old bus about the size of an American station wagon. It was empty except for a few bleeding and fly-ridden dead sheep piled on the roof. We held our noses and Naseeb laughed. "The sheep will be removed at the market in a few miles," he said. "If you sit inside you will not see them. You will not know they are there."

I smiled to myself when I saw the backs of Mimi's legs. I'd never believed that she'd had hepatitis only two months before. Those legs were chubby, sturdy. The Baghdad dates, nuts, rice, and puddings were doing her no harm. She watched to see where Pauline would sit down, then jumped to her side. Pauline was her favorite member of the family.

The rest of us ducked as we stepped carefully onto the splintery floorboards of the old bus. The scene on all sides, once we had left our neighborhood, was wide and tan. Only a few palm trees that danced in the shimmering heat broke the scope of the sandy plains.

Indeed, there were all six of Naseeb's sisters, his mother, brother, and beautiful two-year-old Zuzu. No wonder he was so adored; he had blond curls and eyes as deep blue as delphiniums.

The women wore colorful sarongs. They were warm and welcoming. I was impressed with the all-around air of brightness, both in spirit and dress. A change from Al Waziria, our home outside of Baghdad.

We sat in a large circle in the cool, dark living room, and while the servants passed around cake, fruit, and crackers, Naseeb's mother and sisters regaled us with stories of their flight from Palestine with grim and frightening details. What a strong family, I thought. Here they all were, Mayada, Jomana, Omeina, and the others whose names I wish I could remember, laughing, egging each other on. Their voices were rich and deep. Their Arabic beautiful to listen to even though we didn't understand their words. Naseeb and his brother translated for us. In about an hour, the servant brought coffee, which meant it was time to go.

Alas, we had to leave Joanie there. She was fading fast. The extreme weariness had come over her again. She had looked quite well in the morning. Her color looked bad now, too. My constant worry was, had she contracted the hepatitis germ from her sisters? Naseeb suggested that she stay with his mother and sisters. "They are all like mothers, you know, and I know they will take bedy good care of your daughter." I was reluctant, but we left her there.

Behind the ripples of heat we could see the magnificent arch of Ctesiphon like a god-made sculpture that rose to the sky. Third century A.D., I thought; how many slaves had died in the building of it? Bless the slaves and prisoners who have, through the centuries, left the enduring monuments of the world. Once this was a palace, where the Sultan sat on his dais and ordered wine, food, and his supple women to entertain him with their belly dancing. Where the halls of his harem echoed with the screams of passion, jealousy, and hysterical laughter. What storms, wars, feasts, banquets, death, and corruption that arch had sheltered! Now it was a gathering place for merrymakers on a Moslem holiday or on such a Friday as this.

As we drove closer, the great stone edifice seemed to rise as a part of the flat sands around it, for it was all the same color. We heard drums, singing. There was dancing in circles. Someone trilled a high note and a chorus of rhythmic, thin, bright voices chanted. A circle was formed and the singers and chanters did a tricky step round and round in the circle. Many on the sidelines clapped in rhythm.

I marveled at the dancers in their long black costumes, twirling and swaying in all this heat. It must have been at least 100 degrees. We walked slowly and deliberately toward the Coca-Cola vendor, a youth who leaned against a wall of the giant building just around the corner from the graying old man with a long beard and brown ragged tunic who was selling lemon squash and yogurt.

Naseeb was acquainted with the grounds and he led us to a spot where we could sit in the shadow of the great arch. There we watched for a few moments actually relaxing, feeling free of the fetters of daily routine. Al brought out his camera and while he fixed and focused, there was a sudden quiet. No more dancing and clapping, but a growling mob that stood back from us. Some of the men huddled together and muttered, then glared at Al with stony eyes. Naseeb had gone off for more drinks, but now we saw him striding rapidly toward us. He took Al's elbow, whispering something in his ear. He ushered him away and beckoned us to follow quickly. When we had separated ourselves from the crowd, Naseeb tapped his worried forehead and said, "Dr. Baez, please Sair, put your camera away. This is very dangerous. You see, many people are afraid of them, some have ideas that when you take a picture, you also take away the soul and when there is a mob spirit like this one today, often you see knives flash." Al asked no questions but hustled the source of evil into his bag.

The crowd receded in chattering small groups. It was lunch time. The women opened their baskets of food: sammoun, their bread stuffed with goat cheese, goat meat, bottles of orange juice and lemon squash, watermelons, and grapes. We had brought somewhat the same delicacies, avoiding goat meat.

As the shadow of the arch disappeared under the high noon sun and the sand and sky wrapped us in a hot, white blanket, we gathered our baskets and left the crowds who were settling down for a siesta under the palm trees.

We picked up Joanie, who looked and felt miserable, and drove directly home. We saved our stories of the day for later. But we did tell her about Popsy and the camera. "You know," I said, giving Naseeb a broad grin, "Naseeb saved Popsy's life today."

Looking pleased, Naseeb puffed out his broad chest a few inches. "Oh yes," he said, "I had to save the life of this man. It is bedy important because I must work with him. You know he is the greatest scientist in America and I am the best secretary in all Palesteen."

The Zucs of Baghdad

Al

As the winter approached and the nights became cold, the days were often sunny and warm. The American ambassador once said to me at a cocktail party, "Baghdad is a delightful winter resort." I had never looked upon it that way, but I suppose that if I had not had such an intense sense of mission and had spent a bit more time relaxing at the Alwiyah Club pool I might have felt the same way.

When the weather cooled the seemingly impossible occurred: we actually *enjoyed* shopping in the labyrinth of shops which had seemed so forbidding in the hot days right after our arrival. This marketplace was an intricate network of stalls off Rashid Street. It was an underground world sheltered by palm leaf mats which, in rainy weather, kept most but not all of the rain from dripping into this bazaar called the "*zuc*." A whole section of it was devoted to brass and copper wares. Another to cloth of all kinds. Still another to rugs and carpets, and so on. Our need for things like carpets and food brought us back repeatedly to different portions of this intricate maze.

It had a dirt floor, so the human traffic on it raised clouds of dust that looked like leaning columns—actually shafts of dust illuminated by sunlight that pierced the holes in the matted roof at random. You could not walk in a straight line for more than a few meters before reaching what looked like a dead end but which actually was a T-junction opening up both left and right. You had no idea what was around the corner. New worlds opened up at each turn. We explored different parts of the zucs at different times but we never saw all of it. As far as we were concerned it was infinite in extent.

The first time we ventured forth as a family to the zuc, in search of rugs to throw over the cold tile floors of our house, was on a Saturday so there was no school. If I had been alone I would not have attracted any attention because I could pass for an Arab dressed in western clothes. But my "harem" were conspicuous because its members wore American-style dresses of different colors. Only rarely would you see an Arab woman wearing anything but the long black abayah. My women also stood out because they were exceptionally vivacious and pretty—all of them.

We had been told that one of the many entrances to the zuc was at the copper market on Rashid Street. It could be identified by the huge copper vats, pots, and pans on the street. We got off the bus on Rashid Street near what we had nicknamed "the beat-up old mosque" and walked about a hundred yards south to the place where the copper wares were on display. There was no opening. You just had to push your way past a couple of fat Arabs whose tummies acted like a kind of fleshy turnstile. Suddenly we were under the straw roof that covered the market area. As we became dark-adapted we could see a frenzy of activity. Shirtless and sweaty men were yelling at little boys who operated the bellows that kept their charcoal fires hot enough to heat the copper the men were beating into shape with a hammer. There were several of these fires going on simultaneously and the workers seemed to be competing with one another to see who could make the most noise.

By yelling and making signs we kept asking where the rug market was. A worker would interrupt what he was doing to gape at Joan and the girls and then to point the way. It seemed impossible that there was more to be seen than this huge copper market, but we came to one of these dead ends where we were forced to make a left turn, and lo and behold, here was a completely separate area of this primitive dirt-floor shopping mall. This time it was a vegetable market.

What struck me here was the primitive scale they used to weigh things. It was a simple balance with two pans designed so you could put the weights in one pan and the merchandise in the other—nothing extraordinary about that. But what struck me was their size and their rudimentary nature. The leather straps which supported the pans were about four feet long. The wooden arms to which the straps were attached were about three feet long. Now, I was used to analytical balances with immaculate pans and polished brass weights which are put in place using tweezers. But here the pans, each about a foot in diameter, were dirty and had been banged out of shape by having the weights not placed on them gently but literally thrown on them. The iron weights were rusty and deformed from abuse.

I motioned to the angry looking vendor—they always seemed angry to me—indicating that I wanted to buy some potatoes.

He yelled, "*Biesch*"—how many?

I yelled—and you *had* to yell to be heard—"Nus kilo," which means half a kilo.

Both pans rested on the ground because he had not yet lifted up the arm supporting them. He took the half-kilogram weight and threw it into one pan. It landed with an agonizing thud. Then he dumped an estimated half-kilo of potatoes into the other pan. He lifted the arm supporting the pans into the air to see which pan remained on the ground. It was the one with the weight on it, so he dumped more potatoes, one at a time, into the pan in the air, until the other pan rose off the ground. Then he dumped the potatoes into our basket.

Just to see if he would actually throw a *whole* kilogram weight down on the pan, which would surely dent it even more, I told him, in my broken Arabic, that I wanted to buy another whole kilo of potatoes. His unsmiling face now looked as if he were about to growl, but he went through the whole ritual again, and indeed he did throw the full one-kilogram weight down on the pan from a height of about four feet! It landed with a loud clatter which only added to the ambient din.

"He actually did it," I thought to myself, unable to restrain a smile. It was pure sadism on my part: I was having fun watching him ruin his scales. The vendor still scowled as he poured these potatoes into my straw basket. Only when I paid him did his growl change momentarily into a smile.

At this point a little boy with a sweet face and bright eyes approached us offering to carry the basket. He was in tatters and seemed to be about ten years old, although he was probably twelve. His ragged clothes were dirty, but Joan said he had a face that radiated gentleness.

"He wants to earn some money," said Joan. "Let him carry it."

It seemed mean to let such a little boy carry such a heavy load, but I conceded that Joan was right so I passed the basket on to him and he smiled.

"Me, Jamille," he said. In spite of his size and not very robust frame he lifted the basket on to his shoulder. He knew only a few words in English and we knew even fewer words in Arabic but we communicated with the help of gestures to indicate we were looking for the rug vendors. Jamille motioned us to follow him and we proceeded to walk through other whole areas of this maze. We walked through the cloth market where stall after stall was filled with fabrics of every description, including some plaids which caught Pauline's eyes, as she, in turn, caught the eye of every vendor. Many who were seated as they unfolded their wares would rise to take a second look at her and then at Joanie and Mimi.

"We've got to return some day to buy these plaids," said Pauline. She was the seamstress in our family. She had a gift for sewing professional looking clothes with no pattern at all or from patterns which she would design and cut out of newspaper.

We were now in the rug and carpet area, but it was clear that

Jamille wanted us to go to a special shop so we followed him. He put the basket down and pointed toward an opening which could hardly have been called a door. We had to duck low to enter, and when we did, the merchant rose to his feet and greeted us in a grandiloquent manner. He was dressed in the loose robe-like garment worn by most Baghdadis. None of the merchants in the zuc wore western-style suits—they don't lend themselves to squatting down on the floor. This merchant did not have the angry look of the vegetable vendor. Like a merchant from *The Thousand and One Nights*, he had a shrewd and lively look. We were obviously not the first foreign customers Jamille had brought to his shop.

"Good morning, madame," he said to Joan, and looking at the girls, he said, " . . . and ladies. Please be seated."

His shop could not have been bigger than ten feet square. It was only about eight feet high. Its four walls were lined with carpets neatly folded into bundles which were about two feet long, one foot wide and about eight inches high. Underfoot there were straw mats that covered the dirt floor. A tiny opening in one corner obviously led to a storage area. A single electric light bulb lit his shop. This was absolutely essential because we were in the bowels of the labyrinth where it would have been pitch dark without electric light. The poles that carried these wires were overloaded with the most outrageous patchwork of wires going every which way. They were dust-laden and sometimes bare. I dreaded to think what would happen if they were accidentally short-circuited.

We were anxious to start looking at rugs, but the merchant had already ordered tea for all of us. We could not avoid this ritual. By now we had performed it countless times and knew how to deal with it. A sip or two was all that was required but it would have been uncivilized not to participate.

I gave him my business card which displayed my Unesco connection. From that moment on he addressed me as "Doctor." He didn't say "Doctor Baez." He simply said, "Doctor." He didn't have a card but told me his name was Sharif. Finally, "What can I show you, Doctor?"

"We are looking for some rugs to cover the tile floors of our house here in Baghdad. But we would like them to be nice enough to keep and take home with us when we leave at the end of the year."

"Why do you talk about leaving, Doctor? Baghdad is nice place."

"Yes, it *is* a nice place, Sharif, but I have a permanent job back in California."

"Ah, Doctor, California!" said Sharif. "Marvelous! Hollywood, izzent it?" Baghdadis never pronounce "isn't it" the way we do. They accentuate the last syllable—"Iz-*zent*" and sometimes don't bother to add "it."

"I have exactly what you want," said Sharif. He proceeded to unfold carpets one by one. He held them up by one end and let them unroll dramatically onto the floor—thump, thump, thump. They were all about three feet by five feet. He kept tossing them down and unrolling them in rapid succession, naming them and giving their country of origin as he watched our expressions to see which one we liked.

It was an extraordinary show, and we were all enthralled. The rugs came from Turkey, India, Persia, China, and many other places. Suddenly he threw one down which caught my eye.

"Hold it," I said. "Stop for a minute. I want to look at this one." It was a mulberry red with touches of vermilion. It was subdued and striking at the same time. "What is this one called?" I asked.

"Aha, Doctor," said Sharif. "You have good eye. Is called Bukhara and comes from Uzbek region."

"Beautiful," I said. "Please set it aside. It looks new. Is it?"

"Oh no, Doctor, not new. Very, very old!"

I had obviously committed a blunder. Today, thirty-five years later, this Bukhara rug lies on my bedroom floor looking as new as it did in Baghdad that day.

Sharif then continued his show, tossing carpets down in rapid-fire succession. He was a consummate showman and he was enjoying playing to an appreciative audience.

"How much is the Bukhara?" I asked.

"No money, Doctor, no money. I sell rugs to make friends."

I could see it was going to be difficult to arrive at a price.

"They come from all over the world," I said. "How do you get hold of them?"

"Ah, Doctor, many people leave Baghdad. They sell their belongings before they leave."

Sharif did not mention the Jews explicitly but I had heard that many Jews who had lived in fine homes had been forced to leave Baghdad because of the Arab-Israeli conflict. Before long the rugs had made a pile about a foot deep and we had chosen about five of them of very different kinds but all very attractive. From these we narrowed our selection down to three and began the bargaining procedure. I don't particularly like to haggle, but I had been told that in this part of the world you have to do it. We arrived at a price which I felt I could afford and Sharif folded our carpets into neat bundles, stepped outside of his shop and beckoned his helper, Mahmud, since it was clear that Jamille could not carry everything. We were prepared to carry them ourselves but Sharif said that it would not do for foreign visitors, especially women, to carry anything.

Sharif gave me an invoice which listed my purchases with the numbers written in the Arabic form which was unfamiliar to us. I had been taught in school that the numbers we used in the States are called Arabic numbers, but this was not how numbers were written in Baghdad; one more source of confusion. We had to learn these new symbols quickly, in order not to get cheated.

"Use the rugs for six months. If you no like, bring back. We exchange."

And now Mahmud put the carpets on his shoulders and led the parade which included Joan, me, the three girls, and Jamille weaving our way in the labyrinth through areas we had never seen before but which he obviously knew by heart. Mahmud was long, lean, dirty, and bedraggled. My kids said he was "falling apart." His tattered and ruffled pants came to his knees. He was barefooted. Nevertheless, he was cheerful and had a smile that bordered on silly. He thoroughly enjoyed being watched by the merchants, who obviously knew him.

Soon we were out in the glare and heat of Rashid Street and Mahmud was hailing a taxi for us.

"How much shall we pay him?" I asked Joan as I unrolled my last few fils. Mahmud sensed that I didn't know what to pay him. Verbal communication was out of the question, so he grabbed the few remaining 100-fil notes from my hand. He gave one to Jamille and took the rest for himself, smiling a toothy grin in the process. Jamille looked bewildered but happy. He had never been paid so much for doing so little.

I yelled to Mahmud: "Hey, wait a minute. I need money for the taxi." I grabbed a couple of the bills back from his hand, waving them in the air and saying "For taxi, for taxi!"

Soon all our wares were in the trunk of the taxi and we had managed to squeeze all four of us into the car. It was very warm.

"Al Waziria!" I yelled to the driver above the usual din of Rashid Street and then sat back. We were sweating by now but we looked at one another and smiled, quite content with our adventure and with our loot from the zuc.

Carpets for His Patience

Joan

ALI CONTINUED TO HELP US with the business of living. "Today, Al, I shall get some beds made for us. How many will you be wanting?" Al answered five, and Ali disappeared in a taxi, off to the mattress and bed-framing factory.

The girls and I took a walk down what we called bed-row because we happened on a whole road of ten by ten-foot booths where the small and ageless men, each in his own booth or just in front of it, worked and sweated in long gray dresses and black turbans, hammering, measuring, hand-sawing our bed frames. They were very pleased with their big order. They seemed to know it was ours because they stopped their work for a moment and bowed slightly. "SabbaH el khair, Memsah," they said, and smiled broadly. On down the same road were the mattress factories. There they sat, again two slight men, on their haunches, measuring, cutting, stitching the ticking for our mattresses on an old pedal machine. They, too, smiled and greeted us.

Two days later, a truck limped up to the gate with about a dozen bedframes held together with thick rope instead of springs, and our mattress ticking stuffed with huge lumps of kapok.

Probably the floor would have been more comfortable for

sleeping, but we'd have to deal with lizards, scorpions, and on our roof grasshoppers the length of my hand. Those grass-hoppers managed to jump from the ground to the roof and land on the mosquito netting that I had made to fit and tuck in the beds, leaving two feet of space above the mattress. They bounced happily like a baby in its jump-chair on this netting, until the bounce was all gone, then they hopped to the next bed. This was their territory, and they insisted on their right to live in it. Later we became acquainted with them, held them, and let them tickle the palms of our hands with their sticky pinpoint feet.

Bless Ali. Even if we sat on creaking, hand-woven raffia chairs, ate from wobbly wooden tables, and had to zigzag our bureau drawers open because of the green and swelling wood, we were grateful for his help.

Ali said, "Of course, Al, you will want to buy your Persian carpets, will you not? I know a very fine carpet zuc (market)," and he told us exactly where it was.

So one day we started out on the rickety bus a half mile down the road, bumped our way to another rickety bus and were off to the center of Baghdad via Rashid Street, where mankind turned into a dust-covered calliope in slow motion.

To my eyes it all seemed a hazy brown moving wall of donkeys plodding about, laden with panniers. Sheep in flocks were being driven together by little boys and old men with long sticks, horses wended their way, nose to rump to who knows where, their guides howling "*harra-harra! yella-yella!*" (get out of the way!). Women in black abayahs, many with faces completely covered except for one eye, baby on one arm, shopping basket in the other, pulled their small children behind them. Hairless dogs slunk through the labyrinth of bare feet for morsels of garbage from the gutter, yelping in pain when somebody kicked them mercilessly out of the way. White turbaned sheiks sat in the dim coffee and tea booths passing the time chatting, sipping, and smoking their hookahs while their wives and mistresses bargained for a better watermelon or bunch of spinach for less "*flus*" (slang for fils, money).

The restaurants were opening now, and the pungent odor of frying mutton, *semne* (a butter made from buffalo grease), curry and other spices we knew nothing about permeated the diesel-fumed air and I held my breath and thought, are there really flowers blooming in California?

We stopped in front of a line of open carpet booths, the zuc. Each was individually owned. Some of the owners were sitting together and gossiping; some slept in a shady corner of the booth. We looked for Ali's special shop, the Al Persia.

"Salaam alekum, Doctor," came a deep-throated greeting from the rotund owner of the Al Persia. He bowed politely and his huge stomach pushed against his knees. Yes, he knew we were the Americans coming to look at his rich and ancient carpets, "the best in all Baghdad," he promised us. I think Ali tipped off his merchant friends to be sure we were well treated and that they drove a good bargain.

"I am Hassan," the owner said, offering us wicker chairs and folded rugs to sit on. "Please sit down." In front of us in that twelve by twelve-foot room there were carpets folded and piled to the ceiling along the walls; other piles of them filled every inch of the floor except where we sat. Hassan shouted "Chai!" (tea) in a loud and commanding voice. A white-dressed and turbaned skinny little man appeared, bowed, took orders for three teas, bowed, and was gone. It appeared that we were in for a leisurely chat. Al tapped the arm of his chair with his fingers, cleared his throat and smiled at me, then looked heavenward. Al was being his patient self, but there wasn't much space for more.

"It is bedy nice the weather, Dr. Baez, izzent-it?"

"Yes, very nice," Al agreed.

"Perhaps a little warm for you Americans, I think so?"

"Yes, a little," Al smiled politely, but his lips were rigid.

"And how are conditions in your country, Doctor? Do you have some troubles? Perhaps some poor people there in America, Doctor?"

"Oh, yes we do. I suppose most countries do," Al said, staring at the wall opposite him.

"Hmmm, yes," Hassan looked philosophical, and, I thought, quite the host at this little tea party, as the small man with the white turban bowed his way in with a tin tray and our three-inch glasses half filled with sugar, the top half with tea, and a plate of petite buerre cookies. I thanked God for the cookies—they would help the syrupy tea go down. "I think your wife will have a biscuit?" I took a cookie, thanked the servant who looked away, and I settled in for the morning. Hassan went on, "Yes, Doctor, do you know we have it our troubles too? Poor peoples, many, many poor peoples, but we have it some rich peoples too, many rich peoples, and you know, Doctor, they are bery fine peoples and that is agreeable, izzent-it?" He now offered us a round of cigarettes and as I was definitely not a part of this conversation, I took one, lit up, and listened. Al, of course, refused, but it didn't help.

Half an hour, three-quarters, and Al was looking wiggly. He crossed one knee over the other, then switched, cleared his throat, put down his tea glass a little noisily and said, "Hassan, I wonder if we might look at . . . " his eyes scanned the carpets.

"Yes Doctor, I am happy to show you many, many carpets," Hassan said, and sat back. I thought Al would explode when he offered us another cigarette. I wanted to shout, "He doesn't smoke, you dimwit!" but I didn't, and at that point it seemed that Hassan knew he had played his game long enough. It was time for business. He pulled himself out of the chair that so well preserved his contours. The carpet show was on with all its fine soft textures, religious designs, and rich colors—gold, deep blues, burgundy and purple threads winding through.

"You see, Doctor, all designs are symbols. Here you see the sacred flame of the Zoroaster. Do you see that, Doctor? Some peoples say it is the bend of the river Juma as it leaves Kashmir, but it is the Sacred Flame, I think so. And here in this one is the clenched fist making a seal in blood, bery rich red color, izzent-it? And they are made exactly the same today. Only this one is made in 1792. Bery beautiful carpets, Doctor. Do you like it these carpets?" Al nodded and fingered the velvety softness of the rugs as Hassan unfolded one after another, draping them on the floor and the chairs. "These from Canakkole, a city near the Aegean seacoast in Persia, are made of wool. You will feel the difference in this Anatolian carpet because of the machine spun cotton that was used for the warp. I like it the wool ones better, I think so. This one," he picked out one with an intricate design of gold and red and a deep blue, "you will see is a golden crown. The crown is the symbol of the Persian monarchy in the sixteenth and seventeenth century. Bery beautiful, I think so." Hassan was carried away with the designs, color, and their symbols, while we looked and questioned and wondered which to choose. Hassan loved his carpets as much as we loved our children, I thought!

"Ah," he said, "this one special for Memsah. Yes, bright but bery old colors, beautiful one for Memsah." I was delighted to be noticed, and I thanked him. I had almost forgotten that I was there.

Al said, "What do you think, Joanie?"

"Yes," I said truthfully, "I think it's one of the loveliest," and we chose one after another until we made up five. Al asked, "This bright one—is it new, Hassan?" Hassan pushed his rounded shoulders back and the muscles of his right nostril lifted disdainfully, as he came close to snorting, "*New*, Doctor? Never do I sell it a new carpet. Never!"

Al looked chagrined as he apologized, and then he muttered, "Let's get serious." Al had learned about bargaining and now he had the perfect chance to try his luck. "My wife likes this one, Hassan, how much is it?"

"Aha, bedy good taste, Memsah. She knows it a fine carpet, I see . . . this one is 280 dinars ($784)."

Al slapped himself on the knee and said, "Ha, that's funny. Do you know any more good jokes? I'll give you 150 dinars, Hassan, and that's all."

Hassan looked dramatically crestfallen. "Now I think it you made jokes, Doctor, but for your good wife I make it 200 dinars." And so they went on for what seemed an eternity while I watched with glazed eyes, hoping we'd go home with a couple of carpets, at least; by now I didn't really care which ones. But I saw that Al had chosen five three-by-eight-foot rugs and two hall runners. Now they were shaking hands and laughing. The deals were clinched. Hassan had his money and we had our rugs. Al was completely worn out, but happy. On the way home in the taxi, he laughed now and then about his triumph at bargaining and I relaxed in the thought of our precious purchases.

Mahal, our trusty gatekeeper, all muscle and bone and kindness, opened the gate and there came all his crew: the gardeners, the construction men, and the plumbers, bowing and smiling approval. Jeanne and Ali and their children plus our children greeted us eagerly. They wanted to see our new wares. When we brought out the first carpet and unfolded it, the entire assembly broke into applause. Ali was intent on hearing the details of the financial end of the transaction, and when Al told him some of the prices, Ali's cheek-wrinkles deepened with smiles and he said, "Aha, you know, my friend, today you have become a true Arab." Perhaps that's the highest compliment an Arab can give a foreigner.

Our girls chose and rechose each rug for their very own, and then Al and I dropped on the last two right there on the patio floor and fell asleep.

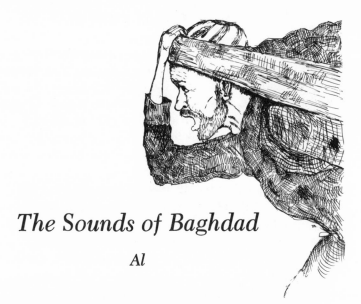

The Sounds of Baghdad

Al

I HAD A FASCINATION for recording sound which I had picked up from my father. This had been his hobby in the late 1920s, even before tape recorders were available, back in the golden days of radio, when sound alone could create a scene in our minds. And so I had lugged a 40-pound reel-to-reel Pentron tape recorder to Baghdad. My plan was to couple the sounds of Baghdad with color slides.

Even during our first bewildering days in Baghdad, I listened with fascination to the sounds we could hear from our hotel room in the Semiramis. During the day it was the piercing and continuous din of the traffic on Rashid Street. This subsided around midnight after which—since we couldn't sleep because of the heat, exhaustion, and uncertainty—we could hear the continuous swell of sound that originated on the other side of the Tigris River. It sounded like dogs barking in the distance and yet there was something different and awesome about the yelps we heard. They created an aura of mystery and fear. We were told later that they were wild jackals in the outskirts of the city. I was then in no mood to start recording sounds. Besides, I didn't even have enough energy to look for the transformer needed to adapt my tape recorder to the voltage of Baghdad.

It wasn't until we moved to our house in Al Waziria, which

was in a relatively quiet neighborhood, that we began enjoying the perspective which distance gave to the sounds of Rashid Street and beyond. From the roof of our house the noise of the distant traffic was no longer threatening. It became just a continuous buzz which subsided around midnight. Then we could hear not only the yelps of the jackals on the other side of the Tigris but also the barking of nearby domesticated dogs competing with their wild relatives.

About 4 A.M. the call to prayer by the muezzin from the minarets of distant mosques began reaching us. Lying in bed, listening to this gentle and reassuring sound and thinking of the faithful who were praying, I felt guilty for not participating. By the time the sun made its appearance over the horizon the sound of the dogs had been replaced by the chirping of birds. You could occasionally hear the distinctive song of a mourning dove or a nightingale, but it was almost drowned out by the continuous chorus of chirps coming from thousands of English sparrows. The effect was noisy rather than beautiful, but it was a most welcome change after a night of barking. Soon the distant hum of bus traffic on Rashid began all over again, punctuated by the honking of taxi horns. North of Al Waziria a distant train ran early every morning and its whistle reminded us of the trains on our western prairie.

When the sun was up the song of the birds subsided and the clatter of neighborhood activity took its place. A vendor passed beneath our window with a huge basket of oranges on his head, yelling, "*Portughal!*"

Our neighbor had a horse whose stable was right next door to my study where I often slept. When he had not been exercised sufficiently he would kick the wall that separated us until I thought his hoof would come through. But when his master rode him up and down the cobbled street in front of our house the cadence of his hoofs against the cobblestones, cushioned by a layer of soil, was melodious. A tattered and barefooted boy vendor, whose dirty clothes seemed to be drenched in the kerosene he was peddling, announced his wares by yelling and banging his gong—the steel casing of an automobile brake assembly—with great vigor. In the rainy weather frogs began to croak in chorus, supplementing the cacophony of sounds that announced the presence of life on our street.

At night a watchman, usually a ragged old fellow who made his living by doing the rounds toting a gun and pretending to protect your neighborhood, would blow a shrill whistle that could awaken the dead. It produced a frightening shriek which sounded like the scream of a desperate soul. In the evening you might be quietly reading in the living room and as he passed under your window he would blow his whistle with a force and a vengeance that would lift you several feet in the air. He might be doing this to let you know that he was on the job or to remind you that you hadn't paid him the fifty fils you owed him.

In the distance you would hear another watchman answering his whistle. They worked in conjunction. If one did not hear the other respond he knew that his partner was not on the job, possibly abducted or asleep.

I captured all of these sounds on my tape recorder by hanging a microphone from our window. They eventually made my slide show come alive.

One night during Ramadan we heard the sound of drums and the singing and wailing of women. I looked over the ledge of our roof, from which I could see up and down the moonlit street. It looked like a stage setting. In the dark we could see a boy doing a sinuous dance. He would twist going down to the ground and then rise up again like a snake. As they got closer and closer, the boom, boom, boom of the huge drums got louder and louder and shook the walls of our house. They were now right beneath us. The boy was writhing in a sensuous way and the women spurred him on with wails and a strange cackling laughter. This was the first time we had seen Arab women having a joyous time—laughing, singing, and playing in the presence of men. They weren't doing the dancing—this seemed to be the men's prerogative—but they *were* having a good time.

I kept recording everything. The intensity of the sound diminished as they moved on but they stopped at a neighbor's house less than a block away. They were going to have a party. Before long they began singing a song in Arabic in unison. It had a catchy rhythm: one, two, *three*—one, two; one, two, *three*—one, two; and so on, over and over again.

All of a sudden the rhythm was picked up by a drum whose deep bass tones made it instantly recognizable as one of the huge drums we had seen and heard at Ctesiphon. They are made by stretching a goatskin over the top of a large clay urn. They are played by striking the skin—and at times the edge of the urn—with a flip of the thumb. The men who didn't have drums kept time by clapping their hands.

Occasionally the rhythm broke and a torrent of sound produced only by the main drummer poured out for about half a minute, which seemed an eternity: ta-ra-ta-ta-*ta*, ta-ra-ta-ta-*ta*, ta-ra-ta-ta-*ta*. This was followed by laughter and a scream. Everything would subside for a while and then the whole sequence would start over again. It went on this way for most of the night and for three nights in a row!

We eventually learned that they had been celebrating the birth of a boy. It if had been a girl there would have been no such celebration. Girls are not wanted in this society, partly for economic reasons. They are not destined to become wage earners. Especially in poor families they are considered a burden. We even heard cruel rumors that in the poorest families girls are sometimes killed at birth.

Ilyas

Joan

I OFTEN HOPPED on the bus that rattled over the dirt road to
Spinney's, the British grocery store about half an hour away.
The bus passed the high cement walls with pointed glass on top,
sealed in to impale unfortunate thieves. Children played in
gutters where there was more sewage than water. Some of
them sat around garbage pails eating orange and banana skins.
Men squatted by the side of the road with their water pitchers.
Having no toilet facilities, they used the gutter and poured
water over their lower section to clean themselves, and then
dropped their long skirts down. Beggars with faces and hands
as brown as the rags they wore leaned on tall sticks or sat with
cupped hands out. We passed mothers, usually pregnant, with
babies and children barely dressed; but no matter what the age,
each one had a nose-ring or earrings of pure gold. Some had
tiny pearls inlaid. Gold was a sign of prestige. Many of the very
poor had their strong white teeth extracted and replaced with
gold. I often wondered how many times they had gone hungry
for that coveted luxury.

Vendors clattered down the dusty way, some with trays of
bread on their heads, calling out "Sammoun, sammoun!" Others
with oranges, called "Portughal helue!" Pushing a home-made
wagon with a huge oil drum nestled in it, the kerosene vendor

shouted "*Nafut, nafut!*" while beating the drum with a husky stick.

I watched the little boys run behind the bus as we bumped along. If they saw me or spied one of our girls, they sprinted fast and beat the bus to the market, greeting us with their straw baskets and cheery faces. "Memsah, me Chris, Memsah. (I'm Christian.)" What they were really saying was, "We'll carry anything for you for big *bakhsheesh.*" I couldn't help pouring out my change into their hands. Nothing made their smiles broader.

Sometimes I found it hard to believe all this—the starving children, the beggars, the filth, the fat sheiks who sat in the bus and smoked, ate oranges, and spat on the floor. The rattletrap bus that surely had square wheels—I always felt bruised in the bottom by the time we arrived. Sometimes I held my breath unconsciously because of the combined smell of diesel fuel and oranges. The Iraqis eat oranges as we drink coffee and, as there are no garbage cans, they drop the peels on the floor. We stepped on them all the way down the aisle of the bus.

The attraction for me in Spinney's store was not the British tinned vegetables and fresh Iraqi bananas and dates, nor the newly slaughtered beef and lamb that filled a glass case with a good supply of brains and viscera, but rather the Syrian clerks who ran the store. I thought them unheralded heroes. They had marched with their families for miles and miles across the desert from Syria to escape persecution. They had survived. They had found a way to live in Baghdad. Now for awhile, I could listen to their dangerous adventures.

I enjoyed flirting with Ilyas, the young man who held the responsible position of Book Clerk. He took his work seriously, even dramatically, sitting on a high stool behind the brass cash register, eyeing the crowd suspiciously. To him every customer was a potential thief. He added the bills efficiently, signing them with the look and sweeping gesture of one who knows. Ilyas was captain in full command of his ship. His face, buried under a shock of wavy black hair, vacillated from snarl to charm as his mood varied. His teeth were blue-white and straight, a vast contrast to the gold fillings of the rich natives and the black hollowed cavities of their servants. All the customers pushed and shoved one another from counter to counter. It was the weighty sheiks with the huge stomachs who formed a solid front line.

I took my time buying the tinned fruits and the newly invented dry milk that tasted like mildew, and the delicious inch-square packages of dates and walnuts, all with the hope that Ilyas would not be too busy to tell me another story. When he had a moment he would motion to me. Then he told me stories of his wretched life as it had been in Syria, and as it was now in the ghetto part of Baghdad. "I have it six sisters, Memsah. All of them sew very good the dresses for the rich Jewish people in the city."

"Jewish people here?" I asked, somewhat surprised.

"Oh yes, very many, but they pay big monies to be here." When he told about them he lowered his voice as if apologizing, and whispered, "My sisters have to do that, Memsah, or they do not eat."

He told me about his faithful friend, Shaabas, who had walked with him all those miles, and whom he had hired to work in the meat section of the store. "He is too old and fat now, Memsah, and he steals too much food for his family, but he is taking care of me for many months and I cannot let him starve."

One day when I arrived at the store, faithful old Shaabas pushed his fat body toward me around and between the well-dressed customers. "Memsah, memsah!" he called. "Ilyas bery sick man, bad sick, maybe he dies today in hospital. He has it big burst appendix, Memsah." He was close to hysteria, he looked frazzled and his apron was various shades of bloody red. His meat surgery technique always left him looking like a wound.

"Where is the hospital?" I asked.

"Too far away on Al Waziria road, Memsah."

"Can I visit him?"

"All people in there dying. You don't mind that?"

"No," I lied. "Show me where. Is it too far to walk?"

He directed me and I left him in front of the great slabs of sheep heads and shanks of beef. I bought some wilted marigolds at a flower booth and tramped down the road where donkeys, camels, and women driving them on with sticks kicked up a brown, dusty fog.

Only about twenty minutes later I saw the low flat-roofed hospital camouflaged in the brown fog.

I felt uncomfortably clean in my light cotton dress as I passed the jaundiced and diseased patients, who lay on mats on the ground, on rickety chaise-longues, or squatted against the brown cement wall with shoulders humped and heads lowered. They were seeking the air that was clearer if not cooler than inside. It was only 9:00 A.M. and already the temperature was 100 degrees.

In sign language I asked a man in hospital garb where I could find Ilyas. He clapped his hands together twice, then shouted at what appeared to be a heap of brown rags. A bent and wrinkled old man stood up slowly and painfully. The pupil of one eye was missing and he had only one brown tooth. He gestured me to follow him through the halls too dark to see anything but moving objects. Gurneys rattled by with a moaning human tragedy on each one.

He stopped at the men's ward that held about 100 beds, each weighted with hopelessness. A rhythmic moaning sounded behind the coughing and spitting that was everywhere. There was a clatter of tin trays, cook pots, and metal dishes. Around the beds hushed sounds like gusts of a light breeze ruffled the air as the women blew flames into the braziers where they cooked their rice and vegetables for the patients they came to see. They sat purdah style on the floor and rocked back and forth as they whispered together. They wept many tears quietly. I had to hold my breath, for the smell of Lysol, defecation, and death was smothering. I couldn't stay long. Where was Ilyas? I saw a limp hand reach up and drop on the gray blanket. There he was, eyes sunken sockets and his face a yellow mask. He stared, tried to smile, then shut his eyes. I came close, whispered hello, and put the flowers on the small table beside him. I realized suddenly that bringing flowers to a hospital was a Western custom and he wouldn't know why I had brought them. I was relieved that the dark room all but hid them.

I whispered close to Ilyas' ear the greetings from his friend, Shaabas, and with a quiet rasp, I heard, *"Ashkurich, Memsah* (thank you)." When I left him, I felt my way between the squatting dark figures in the halls. The old men hobbled on crutches. I felt the hollow stares of many too ill even to see. They were dying, they knew that. It was the only reason to go to the hospital. My body seemed to weigh two hundred pounds as I approached the tall iron gate that led to the road.

As I left the hospital path, an arabana (a horse-drawn four-wheeled carriage) filled with women careened around the corner, going at full gallop. The driver urged them on with shouts of "harra-harra!" and lashes from his long whip. The women wore white veils and gowns. There were too many to fit inside the carriage. They clung to the outer railing and the footstep. Their arms waved and they wailed, keened in high tremolos that sent shivers down my back. A loved one had died and they were opening their grief-stricken souls and voices to Allah, to the sky on their way to the burial ground. Sometimes, for the very poor, there was no burial. They wrapped their dead in heavy white cloth or burlap and left the corpse on a rock far from any dwelling. There the vultures rid it of flesh and the sun bleached the bones.

I thought of Ilyas' family, its poverty. How would they survive without him?

But he lived. Gaunt and weak, Ilyas returned to the store midst applause and laughter in welcome. Slowly, slowly his strength returned until he was able to sit on his pedestal once again in full command of the black account books, his friend Shaabas, and his servant Abdi, who squatted in the corner awaiting his orders. Ilyas now had one more story to tell of his perilous life.

Brickbats and Books

Al

IN BAGHDAD THE MUSLIMS don't work on Fridays because it's their religious holiday. For similar reasons the Jews don't work on Saturdays and the Christians don't work on Sundays. Combine that with the natural desire of people to take an extra holiday, and the result is that in Baghdad, the work week consists of Monday through Thursday. Every weekend is a long weekend. No one seems to mind. But if you don't get your business done by Thursday afternoon you can forget it until about 10 A.M. the following Monday after a round of morning tea.

It is Thursday morning, about eleven. Ahmed the Tall is in my office going over with me the papers needed to clear three trunks full of physics books which Unesco had shipped before my arrival. I have been having difficulty teaching my third-year optics course without a textbook.

The papers are all in Arabic. Ahmed speaks very little English and I speak even less Arabic and I can't *read* Arabic at all. For three weeks in a row, after clearing with my Palestinian student, Hassan Ahmed Hassan, Ahmed the Tall has been going every single day to the Ministries of Education, Foreign Affairs, and Propaganda to get the signatures of approval needed for the removal of my trunks from customs at the airport. Each sheet of paper is about half text and half signatures.

The one thing required of bureaucrats is the ability to sign their names on documents when they are not drinking tea, smoking cigarettes, or chatting. When they are good and ready they sign with a flourish. But they wield veto power and they love to exercise it by refusing to sign if they find anything in the paper that deviates from the rules as interpreted by them.

I now think that our papers are in order and that we'll be able to extract my books from customs today. After a gentle knock, Hassan of the green eyes and curly hair enters my office. As usual, he blushes slightly before speaking: "Good morning, Professor Baez, do you need any help?" Hassan has been awaiting this day because he has become interested in optics and we haven't been able to find any university-level optics texts in Baghdad. He has agreed to prepare a paper on diffraction and is anxious to read some source material on the subject.

"I'm so glad you dropped in, Hassan. Please take a last look at these papers and tell me if anything is missing which would prevent us from taking my books out of customs today."

Hassan checks out every page in the stack and then looks up at me with those green eyes of his. Again, a smile and slight blush brighten his olive-skinned face. "It's all right, Professor Baez. Everything is in order. You should be able to get your trunks out today." He seems as pleased as I because he anticipates getting his hands on the books. My lectures and simple demonstrations on holography have whetted his appetite. Hassan gives some last minute instructions in Arabic to Ahmed the Tall and goes out to hail a taxi for us.

At the customs office Ahmed and I soon find ourselves in front of the clerk who has the authority to release my trunks after he has checked the signatures on all the papers. He does this in a leisurely way, occasionally interrupting his work to chat in Arabic with a fellow clerk at the next desk. Ahmed tries to get him to accelerate the procedure but this is met with a scowl and an explosion in Arabic which I interpret to mean, "Don't tell me how to run my business!"

There is still one hour left before the official closing time of the offices. My expectation of retrieving the trunks rises.

After a meticulous examination of every page, the clerk takes pen in hand and scribbles his signature indicating approval in the appropriate place, hands the papers back to Ahmed, and says in Arabic: "Everything is in order. You may come back next week to pick up the trunks." Ahmed translates this for me. I can't believe it. The moment of release has arrived and due to a whim of this clerk we are once more deprived of our trunks after three weeks of pushing papers around in the ministries of Baghdad.

This is the last straw. I throw up my arms in disgust and storm out of the office into the courtyard. Ahmed is holding the papers and following me. I need to vent my anger somehow. In the middle of the open courtyard I see a pile of bricks that has been left by the workers. Driven by some blind impulse I walk over to the pile. Instinctively I pick up one of the bricks, lift it high above my head and throw it down on the pile with all my might. Crash! The exercise has a wonderful tension-releasing effect. I feel I can use more of the same.

Out of the corner of my eye I see that poor Ahmed is distraught. He can't figure out what has come over me. He probably thinks his American boss has gone berserk over an incident which would not have ruffled the average Iraqi. Why would anyone get excited about waiting one more weekend? I see Ahmed leave in search of the office of the director of customs.

In the meantime a small crowd has gathered. I decide that if throwing one brick has brought me some relief and attention, throwing another will only improve matters. I lift up a second brick from the pile. This time I walk a few steps away from it and toss the brick not *down* on the pile but horizontally *into* it as if I were pitching a baseball into a catcher's mitt. Crash!

Now Ahmed the Tall, all excited, is motioning me to follow him. I feel much better. We enter the air-conditioned office of the director of customs, a noisy, cool haven in a hot desert. Only VIPs have air-conditioned offices. He has a shiny bald head, light skin, beady eyes and a thin mustache. He is wearing a pin-striped suit in an English cut. He is sitting at his desk smoking a cigarette, which has remained in his mouth long enough to produce a cylinder of ash about an inch long. He doesn't remove it from his lips as he starts to speak. The ashes fall onto his lap. This does not faze him.

"Are you Professor Baez?" he asks as he offers me an English cigarette.

"Yes, I am. Thank you, I don't smoke."

"Please sit down. What seems to be the trouble?" I sit. Ahmed remains standing. He is treated as a servant.

"I am very upset because I came to Baghdad at the request of your government to do a job and your bureaucracy seems intent upon keeping me from doing it. You see, I arrived here a month ago to teach physics at the University. In order to do so I need the books which are in my trunks being held here in customs."

"We are under strict orders to censor all books coming into the country, Professor Baez. We are determined to stop the flood of Communist propaganda."

"All of my books are physics books. There is absolutely nothing in them that could be considered propaganda."

By now he has had one of my trunks brought into the office and is opening it, using my keys. He picks up a copy of Harvey White's *Optics* and thumbs through it. He does the same with Richtmeyer and Kennard's *Modern Physics*. The ash from his cigarette, still in his lips, falls into the book. He mumbles without removing the cigarette from his lips.

"Professor Baez, I am going to take an unprecedented step. I am going to release your books, provided you promise to send me a complete list of their titles within a week." At this point he scribbles his initials on the top paper of the pile and motions Ahmed to lock the trunk and carry it out with the help of his farash.

"Next time, Professor Baez, ring my office when you first

receive notification of the arrival of another shipment." He hands me his business card printed in Arabic on one side and English on the other. I figure that if he removed the cigarette from his mouth he might even smile.

We part friends.

School, Yuk!

Joan

THROUGHOUT THEIR CHILDHOOD, whenever someone mentioned school to our children, the response was a resounding *Yuk!* When the first school bus of the season happened by, a miserable "I think I'm going to be sick" came groaning from a bedroom. It meant it was fall, time for school. Alas, there was always school. Even in Baghdad.

We had been in Baghdad for six weeks and it was time to enter the classroom. Why? I wondered. So did the girls. I didn't have the correct parent's attitude, but it seemed to me it was enough to discover the new old world we had just entered on the street, in the stores, the zucs, anywhere but in a classroom.

The girls had already started a small vocabulary in Arabic.

"Mimi, how do you say 'thank you' in Arabic?" our teacher friend asked our six year old one day.

"To a man or to a lady?" Mimi replied.

"Ha," Miss Alaka said, "she knows about that already. To a lady," she continued.

Didn't I burst with pride when Mimi answered, "*Ashkurich.*" She smiled a little shyly.

"But this is very nice," Miss Alaka said. "Now, how about to a man?"

Still with that nice child-like hesitation, Mimi answered, "*Ashkurak.*"

"Perfect!" Miss Alaka laughed with pleasure. So did the rest of us.

Nearly every day, Joanie greeted our old gatekeeper with "SabaH el khair, Mahal." That brought a smile to his leathery old face. Just those little language lessons were a fine starter for me.

History? Almost every time we entered Spinney's store, we had a lesson in history. The men in that British store who waited on us had unbelievable stories to tell us of their flight from Syria to Mesopotamia. We had heard the names of these countries, but they had never meant anything to us. Now it was a different story. They spoke of sultans, kings and heroes; of borders they had crossed; detailing who had survived and describing the terrible deaths of so many of their kin. It was a real-life story to us now.

We tried to learn about buying and bargaining, a lesson I never fully learned. We stopped often to see the men argue, raise their fists, and even spit at one another. One day Pauline and I were under the canopied zuc and a kindly old merchant pulled us into the corner of his booth because there was a bargain battle rumbling. We huddled in the corner and watched the enraged men pick up iron weights and hurl them at each other.

Here were flesh-and-blood beggars, some frightening to look at because they had become mentally deranged from lack of food.

Walking toward us one day was an old man in tatters who held out his hand for fils. When I gave him a few coins, he put them in his mouth and swallowed them. It was no trick. He bowed politely to me, smiled and walked on with his hand out for more.

It took precious little time to discover the attitude men took toward women. A man felt himself undeniably superior to the woman. On the street the man walked ahead of the woman, who trailed him with the heavy wares and usually a baby in her arms. The coffee and tea houses were filled with men; no women were allowed. Nor were women allowed in any restaurant except a certain cocoa shop on Rashid Street. There a woman or a girl could sit on a chair or a bench, not on the sidewalk. The rich sweet smell of cocoa lured us in there often. Women in there peeked at us through their veils.

What an education our kids were getting about the rich and the poor! Here we were living well in a poor section of town where children ate from our garbage pail and their homes were low-built mud huts. The little girls rose early in the morning and wandered over the fields to pick up dried cow chips so the mothers could make fires to bake an early batch of sammoun. Many of the small boys stayed in the marketplace to carry the foreigners' baskets, show them the shops, and hope for a generous tip.

It was quite another story the day an Iraqi statesman invited us to his mansion for dinner at the other end of town, the South Gate. We saw with full impact the breadth of the gap between the rich and the poor. We drove past mansions built of stone and marble. We walked on Persian carpets down the dusty road from our host's wrought iron gate to his home. Trees of roses led to tropical gardens and we sat in the tall-ceilinged living room on pink velvet couches, stared at the luxurious marble tables and the carved marble mantelpiece with ancient brass, silver, and copper objects on top. The objets d'art were jumbled. There were wooden elephants, carved wooden minia-ture men, brass goblets, iron candlesticks, and I even spotted a pink plastic horse hidden behind a silver feather fan. Pauline sat next to me and I watched her enormous eyes drinking in the sights, but never a comment until I spied four huge barrels at one end of the room. I asked a member of the party what they were for.

"These, Memsah," he threw his voice around the room, "these are many precious cups from all over the world." He allowed me to make a small gasp of surprise, then, "Oh yes, Memsah, Sahib collects beautiful antique china from everywhere. He has just returned from his holidays and these are a few of his new collection." With a sweeping gesture of the arm he strutted away.

Pauline waited until he was out of hearing distance, then whispered, "I guess old saw-hips struck it rich." Saw-hips meaning Sahib, of course.

The girls vividly remembered two things about that visit. One, they looked forward to the movie old saw-hips was going to show them (but he didn't), and the other was a four-by-ten-foot fish tank encased in the two-foot wall that separated two rooms. Beautiful tropical fish swished their butterfly tails and blinked bubbly eyes that were the color and size of children's glass marbles.

Two claps of the master's hands and a turbaned, barefoot servant appeared, out of the wall it seemed, to offer me a cigarette and to light it. Rich and poor, poor and rich, a division wider than the country itself. Wasn't that education enough?

NEVERTHELESS, I AGREED reluctantly to help Al find a school. We found only one where English was spoken, but perhaps it would be fine. It was an Iraqi orphanage on one side and on the other a French convent run by British nuns. The buildings were separated, but it was all run by the same people. Good. At least our children would make some Iraqi friends and perhaps learn a little of their language and customs. That was our hope, but the Iraqi children didn't go to school as far as I could see. They stayed in their building learning how to be servants. I saw several of the girls one day when I peeked in the door. In their gray, baggy dresses and bare feet they swept down the stairs, scrubbed the cement floor, and swept the pathway with palm fronds. So thin, wide-eyed and scared looking, I thought. I smiled at one of them. She looked startled and turned away.

We made an appointment at the other side of the school where only the children of diplomats and statesmen were allowed.

The five of us entered the dark and somber office that smelled of stale incense. Dreary, brown-framed pictures of Christ on the cross hung on the walls, and I heard the sound of jingling beads coming toward us down the hall. For a moment I had a terrible sense of panic as I remembered the nightmare months my sister and I spent in a convent in the U.S. midwest when we were children.

We enrolled (enlisted would be more appropriate) the girls with Mother Gabriel, who sailed into the office like a large white albatross. Her stiff white headgear stretched wide on either side of her head. Starched white to the feet, she was efficient, cantankerous, and practically blind. She held out an arthritic hand to shake ours and said, "Dr. Baze and children, good morning."

Mother Gabriel spoke in clipped, short sentences, mentioning the check she was to receive and the date several times. She leaned down the desk until her thick glasses practically touched the paper as she wrote out the bill. Her lips puckered into what was probably meant for a smile as she handed the girls some books and a list of the rules. Then with an almost threatening glance at Al, she handed him the bill. At that moment, I wished her winged headgear would fly her right out the window.

"I'm sure your children will make a fine record for you, Dr. and Mrs. Baze." She opened the door then, and bade us farewell. On leaving, I realized that my knees were shaking. The whole scene had stirred up horrible memories of long ago. I felt I ought to say something now so the kids wouldn't have to go through possibly an unforgettably harsh few months. Maybe I was being too soft. . . . I couldn't decide, and unfortunately, I said nothing.

When the girls came home from school, the conversation and stories were stabbed with vitriolic sarcasm.

"Old pink-cheeks almost got me when she threw the eraser, but I ducked. She caught me crossing my eyes at her," Pauline said, and laughed angrily.

Mimi sobbed, "And she threw my writing book on the floor because I didn't know what dictation meant." More sobs, "I was afraid to pick it up because I thought she'd hit me." Then Joanie made her laugh by waddling around the room, elbows flapping and making a fish-face.

"Mimi, here's Sister Rose," she said.

It sounded like a Charles Dickens' classroom scene to me. I didn't encourage their behavior, but I let them talk, and secretly hoped they'd all be expelled. When I told Al about them, he looked sorry and said, "Oh dear, poor things," and then went back to work.

Discipline on the bus was rigid. "No talking, no talking, and keep your hands off those curtains," Joanie said, imitating the Sister in a shrill voice that sounded like fingernails on a tin pot. "That's Sister Ann. I hate her."

I didn't understand why the curtains on the bus had to be closed—whether the girls shouldn't see how things looked on the streets or people out there shouldn't see the faces of young foreign girls. One day one of the students did open the curtain for a peek, and she gasped at what she saw. Sister Ann rushed to the window, but it was too late. The curtain was wide open by then and everybody stared in horror at the scene outside. The bus was at the North Gate. There, extended from a rope strung across the market square, tied up in mud-splattered sheeting, were four men hanging. Killed in the night. We never found out why. Possibly a robbery or some political reprisal.

"We were all scared," Pauline said, "and everybody got quiet and kind of shaky." Joanie wasn't there that day, but the other two girls felt a shiver run down their spines every time we drove through that square.

Whether on the bus or in the classroom, Mother Gabriel was rapidly losing patience with our belligerent trio, and one day the phone rang, with a rasping British voice at the other end of the wire: "Mrs. Baze, you and your husband are to be in this office in one hour!" It was the Mother Superior.

"Trouble?" I ventured, shakily.

"Indeed there is trouble," she barked.

I told her we'd make an appearance sometime during the day. I called Al and we claxoned our way by taxi to what I called the Gull's Cave. "Are you worried?" Al asked me.

"Well, I hope they haven't been too active. They hate the place so."

"Don't worry," he said, with a kind of confidence that comforted me.

The three girls sat on a long wooden bench in Mother Gabriel's office. They looked submissive, but dangerously giggly. Al and I watched and listened to the enraged Mother, who was panting after an hysterical outburst.

"What does this disgusting note mean?" she crackled. "Who honks like a goose and has a face like a moose? If that's what you teach your children in the name of poetry, Dr. Baze, then I'll have none of it! And . . . " She turned to Sister Rose, who stood behind her, pink hands in pious position, just above her stomach, her face an apoplectic red, " . . . and this!" Mother took a rumpled note from Sister Rose's hand. Now there was an unmistakable rise in tension. The three girls' heads all but submerged into their chests. They shut their eyes and tightened their lips together, shoulders high, and I thought, God help them, what now?

Mother Gabriel rasped out, "What is a woofie?"

Is there a child in the world who doesn't enjoy the performances of our bodily functions, rally to the sound of a good burp, or a healthy gastronomic breaking of wind? The very words associated with their natural actions never failed to send our girls into a state of teary-eyed hysterics. I used to ask them, why was it all so funny? The answer was, we don't know, it just is. To think I missed so much fun in my sterilized upbringing and I was surprised that Al didn't have my somewhat pure and disdainful attitude toward both word and action. In fact, it was he who invented an easy substitute for the controversial verb *to fart*.

"Oh," he said, "what's wrong with a woofie?" when the girls were trying discreetly to say that Sister Rose was guilty of the natural function. The word became a cherished household secret, and Popsy was given some respectful credit.

"Well?" Mother demanded. Silence couldn't have been noisier. I saw the back of Al's neck and watched his ears rise half an inch. He cleared his throat, leaned across the desk, jutted his face forward, met eye to eye with Mother, and said, "Mother

Gabriel, children have their own language and I'm not inter-ested in what you think about it. Neither am I interested in your tantrums. I am withdrawing my children from your school as of today."

Across the room three faces lifted and all eyes flashed a loving glance at Popsy, who hadn't let them down. Mimi's legs swung with triumph under her chair. The other two girls suppressed their smiles. Mother Gabriel's face turned to pink stone. The white albatross was losing the battle. She looked distraught, minus her authority. She had to think quickly. She needed our good dollars. She changed her tack and her face. "Not at all, not at all," she smiled plastically. "The past is over. We'll turn over a new leaf and start a clean page, won't we, girls?"

Not a word from them. Their lips were shut tight, still holding down the rising urge to giggle. We agreed to keep them in school on a trial basis and we managed to get out the gate before the cork popped and there was a raucous outburst of laughter. Popsy had neither scolded nor questioned. He squeezed Mimi's arm in a loving way and said, "How do you like that?"

By Christmas, Pauline had studied enough about the beat-out old British kings, as she called the past heroes of the British Empire. Mimi had shed too many tears over her red-marked notebooks and the humiliation of being the object of Sister Rose's sarcasm. Joanie gave way to a severe case of hepatitis. And so, to their combined happiness and mine—I wasn't sure about Popsy's—we withdrew them from school for good.

ABOVE: Joanie near Unesco Headquarters in Paris.

BELOW: Pauline, Joan, Joanie, and Mimi at the Place de la Concorde.

ABOVE: The fourteen-fils bus on Rashid Street.

BELOW: The ten-fils bus at Bab-el-Muatham.

ABOVE: Arab children on Rashid Street.

BELOW LEFT: The tea vendor near the bus stop. BELOW RIGHT: Fresh-baked sammoun every morning.

ABOVE: A labor-intensive approach to house-building in Al Waziria.

BELOW: Home, shared with Ali Kamal family.

ABOVE LEFT: Mahal, gatekeeper and construction foreman.
ABOVE RIGHT: The beggar who swallowed coins.

BELOW: Christmas goodies for our neighbors.

ABOVE: Construction of the physics lab begins.

BELOW: Albert the Armenian supervises the painting of the lab.

ABOVE: Amelda, Ahmed the Tall, and Shauki stage mock experiments in the completed lab.

BELOW: The finished lab tables and the stored equipment in the newly constructed cabinets.

ABOVE: Abandoned engineering dorm soon to become science labs.

BELOW: The unofficial group portrait, with Dean Duri caught laughing.

ABOVE: Our private bus to Ctesiphon.

BELOW: The arch at the ruins of Ctesiphon.

Above: Plaid pants fashioned by Pauline.

Below: View from the roof of our house in Al Waziria.

ABOVE: Tally-Ho!

BELOW LEFT: The Royal Hunt Club Party. The Regent of Iraq at extreme left. BELOW RIGHT:Pauline is awarded the brush. Mr. Badee (left), the Master of the Hunt (right).

ABOVE LEFT: Tasty oranges all winter long. ABOVE RIGHT: Captain Pudding's servant being risque, showing her bare arms.

BELOW: The mosque at Khadhimain.

Building the Physics Lab
Al

I MET MOHAMMED SHUKUR at a cocktail party. He was the general manager of the Iraqi Bank. He had taken me for an Iraqi and was surprised to learn that I was an American working as an international civil servant for Unesco. He spoke English perfectly with a British accent.

"What is the nature of your assignment here, Professor Baez?"

"Well, I am a physicist and am here as the chief of a Unesco mission whose task is to teach the basic sciences and establish science departments at the University of Baghdad."

"But there is no University of Baghdad, Professor Baez."

"So I have learned. Strictly speaking you are correct, but I am teaching at the College of Arts and Sciences, which is supposed to be the nucleus of the future University of Baghdad."

Shukur was a dark, urbane looking Arab dressed like a British businessman. He lit up at the mention of the college. "You know, there was an Egyptian physics professor at the college last year who ordered a lot of equipment."

This took me by surprise. I had heard of Professor Nooh but had begun to doubt his existence. He was expected back this year but the semester had started two months ago and no one had heard from him. People simply said, "Oh, the Egyptians always arrive late."

I said, "It is interesting you should mention the equipment. No one at the college has been able to tell me where it is. No one seems to know."

"Well, *I* know where it is," said Shukur. "The Iraqi Bank handled the financing of its purchase. The equipment itself was entrusted to the Iraqi Bank for safekeeping until such time as a physicist at the college could identify all those items whose names mean nothing to any one else. As general manager of the bank I am responsible for it. The boxes are sitting in our warehouse. I would be happy to turn it over to you once we get the authorization to do so from Dean Duri."

And that was how I discovered the location of the equipment. It fell in line with my experience thus far that everything of importance to my work and my life in Baghdad would be discovered by accident. That's how I had found a house, my first-year students wandering about the halls of the college, and books for them at the USIS.

After a series of maneuvers that were almost as energy consuming as getting my books out of customs, I managed to have all the equipment transferred from the bank to the college. There was no place to store it so it was put in the auditorium. The chairs were pushed aside on its tile floor and soon we were opening boxes and cataloging their contents. An advanced student from the law school was assigned to me as equipment clerk. He knew nothing about physics, but he was next in line for a government post and the job of equipment clerk for physics at the college was the first to open up.

His name was Shauki. He was very dark, had heavy eyebrows and a generous mustache, walked with a slight stoop, always wore western clothes, and had a warm smile. I liked him immediately. He was very respectful. He realized that he knew nothing about physics equipment but was determined to learn. He appreciated very much the fact that I assigned my bright student Hassan Ahmed Hassan as his advisor on matters of physics. He had access to the catalogues which listed and described each piece of equipment and he pored over them with the diligence of a lawyer examining the evidence for a case. He was given full responsibility for the equipment, and he took this assignment very seriously.

I had told Dean Duri that although I had many bright students who did well in theory, they were all very weak in the experimental and practical aspects of the subject. In fact "practicals" was the term— of British origin— used in Baghdad for what we Americans call "lab work." The Iraqis had had essentially no lab work.

"You know," I had said to Dean Duri, "the most important contribution I could make while I am here would be to set up a well-equipped physics teaching laboratory. If I could do that my stay in Baghdad would have been worthwhile."

And Duri had said to me, "Right you are, Professor Baez. The government of Iraq has set aside 150,000 dinars for this purpose." That would have been the equivalent of close to 450,000 US dollars at the time. But neither the Dean nor anyone else was able to tell me how to get access to those funds. I began to despair. We had no place to put the equipment I had found so that it could be used for actual experimental work.

On another social occasion I ran into Professor Ritchie, the Canadian who was the Dean of the School of Engineering. He told me there was an abandoned dormitory of the School of Engineering about three blocks away from the College of Arts and Sciences and that he was quite sure I could be given access to it. I jumped at the chance of using it as a temporary lab. Details were discussed between the two deans and soon Shauki, with the help of students like Hassan, began moving selected pieces of equipment from the auditorium to the old engineering dormitory three blocks away. We began doing some experiments there by using the large boxes in which the equipment had arrived as tables. We borrowed a few chairs from the main building. The students even used the tile floor itself instead of tables.

The security implications of the set-up were serious, and Shauki, who was the only one who had keys to the dormitory building and its rooms, did not allow any one else to use them. He once said to me: "If any of this equipment is stolen, I will be held responsible and will go to jail."

As time passed I began to lose hope that any of the 150,000 dinars would ever become available to me. I felt, once again, that I had to do something drastic to awaken the authorities. So I wrote a letter to Unesco in Paris saying that I had reached an impasse. I told them that neither the Dean nor the Minister of Education had taken any steps to implement the construction of a lab and that I felt it was useless for me to stay on in Baghdad. The construction of a lab, I wrote, was the most important step to be taken if our mission was to have any real impact. If no action was forthcoming I would be ready to drop everything and leave. I sent a copy of my letter to Dean Duri and another to the Minister of Education.

This action had the desired effect. Dean Duri called me at once into his office. "You should not have sent a copy of this letter to the Minister of Education, Professor Baez."

"I'm sorry, Dean Duri," I said. "I was desperate. I have been here over two months and nothing has been done about the construction of science laboratories. The one thing all students in science in Baghdad need is actual contact with instrumentation. The knowledge they are getting is too theoretical. What's more, you have repeatedly told me that 150,000 dinars have been set aside for laboratories but no one can tell me how to latch onto any of it."

"Right you are, Professor Baez," said Duri, lighting his pipe. "I will speak to the Minister of Education about this tomorrow."

That very afternoon, however, I received a phone call from the Minister or Education summoning me to come to his office downtown. "Professor Baez," he said, "we have not met. You should have made an appointment to meet me as soon as you arrived."

He was right, of course, but my knowledge of protocol was deficient and I had spent so much of my time in finding housing for my family, books for my students, and equipment for experiments that I had had no energy left over for protocol. But he was also playing a game. He was putting the blame on me when, by rights, he and the other authorities who had requested and obtained technical assistance from Unesco should have treated the Unesco team of Mohler, Wilcinski, and Baez with more diplomatic deference.

The Minister continued, "You should not have written Unesco about money for the laboratories. The problem you have raised is an internal one. Money for laboratories has been appropriated but it will take time before it becomes available."

"I am very sorry to disturb you," I said, "and I apologize for writing to Unesco about it, but, technically speaking, I am a member of a Unesco team and must write periodic progress reports to Unesco."

The phone rang and the Minister picked up the receiver to answer it. He also managed to light a cigarette and put it into his mouth where it remained throughout the rest of the conversation. This was a behavior pattern I had now seen several times among higher officials. The Minister kept saying, "*Ei*," "*Na'am*," or "*Beli*" over and over again—different ways of saying "Yes." Occasionally he would shake his head and the ashes from his cigarette would fall to the floor.

The interval gave me the opportunity to pull out a list of needs for converting one floor of the engineering dorm into a modest but well-equipped physics lab and seminar room. I had visited Father Connell at the Baghdad College and seen his marvelous lab. Father Guay, another Jesuit priest, and Father Connell had designed their own lab after considerable study of available construction materials in Baghdad. They had, for example, designed the supports for the lab benches along the walls using brick instead of wood because bricks were cheaper and more readily available. They had offered to lend me their blueprints and gave me the right to copy anything I wished from them.

When the Minister had finished his phone conversation he said to me, "What would you need to get something done this year?"

"We could convert one of the large rooms in the old engineering dormitory building into a physics laboratory and build cabinets for the equipment for a minimum of 1,200 dinars," I said offering to show him my list.

He didn't bother looking at it but called in a young engineer named Alaka and assigned him responsibility for helping me to get the materials and workmen necessary to do the job. The next day the Dean received a check for 600 dinars as a down payment with a promise to send the balance in due course.

Work got started immediately on the construction of cabinets and the brick supports for the benches. Most of the handwork I had seen in Baghdad was of very poor quality but the carpenters who built the cabinets and the plumber who installed the sinks were quite skilled. Alaka would give them verbal instructions and very sketchy drawings. They were not used to following blueprints. Alaka came by every day to supervise their work. He never touched anything. In this society that was beneath him. He was always impeccably dressed in a suit of English cut. As a Christian who had studied engineering in the United States, he treated me with respect and I reciprocated. As an engineer he understood the importance of what I was trying to do, namely, to infuse scientific education with an experimental approach. He also respected my wishes to install the wiring in the lab so that it was hidden. Normally wires were nailed into the walls after the painting was complete, giving the room an unfinished appearance.

An Armenian Christian by the name of Albert was hired to supervise the painting of the walls and the ceilings. We became very good friends. He was a very competent painter. He no longer did any of the painting himself but he came in almost daily to supervise the mixing of the paints for the walls to make sure it produced the soft green color I had chosen. His crew worked rapidly and well.

Albert had painted the Regent's Royal Bilat and in his work for us he gave us the "royal treatment." He understood what I was trying to do and took pride in making a contribution to the establishment of a laboratory. It took him and his crew several weeks to finish everything, so we still had to conduct labs in the other empty rooms of the dorm, but now I knew that when I left Baghdad there would be a place for students to do experiments and where equipment could be stored safely. My students now did not mind working in the other bare rooms, knowing that something better was in the offing.

During the winter months before the new labs could be used, it got pretty cold in the empty rooms where my students were trying to perform experiments under the direction of Sue Gray al Salam, an American woman physicist from the University of California who had married an Iraqi mathematics professor. It was so cold they had difficulty manipulating the equipment. They would keep blowing into their hands. I was dismayed. Several weeks earlier the Dean had promised to send six kerosene Primus stoves to the lab.

I had a single stove in my office in the main building three blocks away. I took it to the lab. I then phoned the Dean and asked him if he would stop by my office on his way home, and we agreed on a time. I was ready, wearing my overcoat and sitting at my desk when he entered.

When he walked in he said: "Professor Baez, it's cold in here. Don't you have a stove?"

"It *is* cold, Dean Duri," I said, "but I took my stove over to the physics lab because it's even colder there, and my students have difficulty in handling the equipment."

The next day I had my stove back and there were six new stoves in the physics lab.

AS THE SCHOOL YEAR progressed and I became more and more immersed in my work at the college, I relied on Joan to carry the burden of caring for the children and their needs. It was difficult enough for her to do the shopping for food and the cooking but with the advent of Joanie's illness she had to cope with that as well. This meant more trips to the doctors and a search for the medicines prescribed by a battery of specialists Ali had brought in to "help."

One afternoon, when I was getting ready to leave the house to return to the college after my siesta, Joan saw me in the corridor and said, "Abo, you only rested about twenty minutes. You're going to get terribly tired. What's more, it's still very hot out. You know how heat affects you. And you know very well that nobody else will be up and around at the college."

She was right on all counts but I was driven by a burning desire to see my laboratory construction job successfully concluded before we left Baghdad, and the time seemed to be flying. Everything moved more slowly than anticipated. So, I couldn't sleep any longer.

The work at the college kept me running. It made me think of the Bud Schulberg novel *What Makes Sammy Run?* As I walked along Rashid Street and saw tea house after tea house full of Arabs in their long robes playing checkers, smoking a hubble bubble, sitting and sitting and twirling beads for hours on end, I thought of a title for a book: *What Makes Ahmed Sit?*

Why did I work while so many Arabs sat? Why did I cut my siesta short to get back to the lab when in order to enter the lab I had to wake up the farash who was sleeping on the floor outside?

I was determined to leave a well-equipped laboratory where students could do experiments. It would be a place where the measuring instruments—electric meters, calipers, thermometers, analytical balances, and stopwatches—would be available to give them numbers. These numbers, derived from experiment, give operational meaning to the fundamental quantities of physics: mass, length, time, electric charge, and so forth. They would enable the students to verify the formulas in their textbooks, rather than simply memorize them, and to clarify concepts which would otherwise remain fuzzy and theoretical.

Joan saw me to the door and kissed me goodbye as I walked out of the house into the hot and dusty street. On such days the farashes covered the windows of the college with screens made of palm leaves which they doused with water. This had a cooling effect on any slight breeze that might go through them. I did, indeed, have to waken the farash who was guarding the front door of the lab. Alone, I was able to survey the progress being made by plumbers, carpenters, and electricians.

This afternoon the first one to return was Amelda, the young woman who had been assigned to help Shauki as the main caretaker of the physics laboratory and its equipment. She seemed disconsolate.

"How do you like your job, Amelda?" I asked.

She hesitated, began to respond, and instead began to sob.

"What's the matter, Amelda?"

When she regained her composure she said, "I like my work, but it's Shauki; he treats me like a slave." This was not difficult to believe. In the Arab world of that day women were treated as inferior beings even though by law women had the right to hold positions in the university and according to the newly developing customs women did not wear the black abayah while they were within the college grounds. Still it was difficult for men to break away from long-held traditions.

When Shauki came to the lab I called him aside and spoke to him about this matter. Shauki was very dark and good looking, with a black mustache which sat very well on him. He took his responsibility at the lab seriously, but he broke out in a warm smile whenever he spoke with me. He sensed that a feeling of mutual respect existed between us. I decided it would be best to speak first with him alone, because he might have felt humiliated if I had called in Amelda at the same time. But after I had explained to Shauki my perception of Amelda's role, which he was able to accept, at least intellectually—they were both law students in the same grade—I told him that I wanted to speak to both of them together. I called Amelda into the room.

Shauki held me in such high regard that he was able to take from me advice which he probably would have rejected from anyone else. Amelda was by nature timid. She held her head low during this meeting, but it was clear that she was pleased by my intervention. I can't imagine that this talk changed Shauki's innermost feelings, but for the rest of the year Shauki and Amelda worked well together.

With the support of the Minister of Education and the day-by-day help of Mr. Alaka, the engineer whom he had employed to oversee the work, we began to see cabinets and workbenches built and gas, water, and electrical outlets installed, all with a minimum of external wires showing and no unsightly nails in the walls.

The construction of benches and tables and the painting of the labs would not be finished until the last week before my departure; but as the work progressed, the students, who still had to work in improvised settings, began to peek in daily to see the changes that were taking place. They seemed pleased.

They treated me in a friendly but very respectful way. They smiled when I said "*SabaH el noor*" (good afternoon) and they returned the greeting in spite of my mispronunciation. My minimal Arab vocabulary also included the words for water (*mai*), gas (*ghas*), and electricity (*carabah*).

My third-year Palestinian student, Hassan Ahmed Hassan, had taken on the role of laboratory instructor on a volunteer basis, partly to help me, since Shauki knew no physics, and partly to gain some experience in performing experiments. He realized he was weak in that area, even though he was brilliant in theory.

The students had very little knowledge about the relative costs of laboratory materials. I questioned them about the cost of the voltmeters and ammeters they were using, and it was clear that they didn't have the foggiest notion about it. They gasped when I told them that a voltmeter cost 15 dinars. This was what Shauki received as a monthly wage. I explained to them that if a voltmeter were damaged it would have to be sent all the way back to England to be repaired at great cost and loss of time. Their appreciation and respect for the lab and its contents began to grow.

Once one of the students accidentally pushed a beaker off the table and onto the hard tile floor where it broke with a crash. The student immediately went in search of the farash and ordered him to sweep it up. I intervened and said that in this laboratory the student responsible would get the dust pan and brush and clean up the mess himself. Whereupon I started to illustrate my point by doing it myself.

This produced sounds of indignation; the students considered it undignified for a professor to be doing this. I explained, however, that if I had been doing research in my own laboratory and had had a similar accident I would not hesitate to clean up my own mess.

An American Thanksgiving

Joan

ALI STRODE INTO the forty-foot-long living room looking pleased as a puppy with a bone. "We must have an American Thanksgiving for our American friends," he announced, in a spirited voice.

"Oh, Ali," groaned his gentle wife who was pregnant and tired most of the time. Sometimes the heat alone wearied her. She slumped low in her chair. "Oh Ali, honestly."

"Well, my dear, I think this would be very nice." Ali loved to eat as much as he loved his wife; and after all, wasn't she there to provide the homey touch for him?

There would be no thanks and no giving. It was to be food all the way, and, at the center, Tom Turkey, of course. Ali said he would be delighted to buy one. It would cost the equivalent of one American dollar. He would pay for it himself and we could do the rest.

The day before Thanksgiving, Jeanne and I boarded the rickety bus to the market about two miles away. We each carried two large baskets. At the market we beckoned two of the ragged little boys who waited interminably for the rich foreigners to ask their help. They were light-footed, they knew the markets, they bargained well, and their brown eyes snapped when they smiled. They would bring us the best of whatever we wanted from every cubicle: fresh vegetables, rice, dates, potatoes, pears, melons of every variety. Each time they returned with something we had requested, there was that wide smile that showed strong, white teeth. God had certainly favored the Arab people with beautiful teeth.

The air was hot and full of dust. There was a dead rat smell wherever we went, but the boys never gave up. "Memsah like? Memsah want?" A nod from one of us and their faces became bright with the joy of accomplishment. They were off then for the next item. The part they liked, and I must admit so did I, was the bakhsheesh. I think there's no smile greater in the whole world than that of a little boy who's receiving the money he's just earned. They earned their pittance, although I neglected to heed Ali's warning, "Don't give them too much. They are easily spoiled. They can manage."

We left our barefooted friends at the gate, staggered into the kitchen with our burdens, and pushed what we could into Jeanne's beautiful Kelvinator refrigerator.

The kitchen was bare except for the fridge, the three-burner kerosene stove, a sink with cold water tap, and now a new sink-board that was a planed-down slab of wood one foot square held up by a stick cemented to the tile floor, plus an Arab prayer. Pots and pans stood in disarray in the corners.

Jeanne was too weary to stand, she sat on the floor and mixed two teaspoons of Nescafé with some powdered milk. "I'll just put the kettle on to boil, and let's have some coffee," she smiled up at me. We dragged ourselves out to the back verandah, sat in the shade, and discussed plans for the momentous day.

We started early Wednesday morning. We scrubbed the vegetables in permanganate water. We foreigners were wary of the dubious fertilizers that had accompanied them in the growing; some said it was human. We took no chances. We cut celery roots and onions, mixed them with sammoun, the native bread, and our own home spices. We soaked them in a powdered milk mixture to leave overnight. Stuffing for Tom. We washed the spuds and yams, picked pebbles out of the rice, shelled pistachio nuts and almonds, washed cantaloupes, oranges, and bananas in permanganate. Then we tucked them away for tomorrow's feast. We took coffee breaks now and then, splashing cold water on our faces—the day was terribly hot. We finished the preliminaries at about tea time. Jeanne looked tired.

Thanksgiving morning we were in the kitchen before the sun was up, our sleeves rolled, ready for action, and in walked Tom Turkey. He looked as startled as we did. Jeanne muffled a scream. "Mahal, do come here!" Mahal appeared. Not only was he our gatekeeper, guard, cement-mixer, painter, plumber, now he was our butcher. His eyes were red and filmy. What was left of his hair was hidden under his turban except for a few wisps of gray that stood out like straws in a hay field, and his two golden front teeth were plainly visible when I motioned that Tom's head had to be severed. There was an evil glint in those red eyes when he picked up the fluttering bird, folded him under his arm, and disappeared. Jeanne disappeared in the opposite direction. I heard a raucous squawk—Tom had met his doom. I hustled nervously about, wanting neither to listen nor to think.

Mahal appeared holding the bird, neck to the floor dripping blood. *"Mai, Memsah, mai."* He needed hot water for the plucking and after motioning him and his still-jumping feathered friend out the door in as gentle a manner as possible, I heated water and marched out to the back porch.

Mahal was hunkering, Arab style, on his haunches, in our coffee corner, grinning and plucking. Feathers flew in all directions. Some raw-necked vultures on the stone wall flapped their wings, strained their necks forward, and blinked their beady eyes eagerly. They had already done away with Tom's head and they knew there was more coming.

Within an hour Mahal was back in the kitchen caressing a bloody, blueskinned, denuded bird. He looked triumphant as he tossed it in the sink. Jeanne and I had made sure that all surfaces were bloodless. Now to the viscera. While Jeanne went out to tend her children, I attacked.

Chickens are one thing to gut out. Turkeys are something

else. Their muscle, tendons, and nerves are like nylon elastic. They give, but they don't let go. I reached in beneath his still warm nub of a tail, crooked my fingers around the invisible wet strings and spongy bumps, bloodying my arm to the elbow. I then placed my left hand firmly across his body, balanced myself with legs astride, and started pulling—gently at first, then more vigorously—until my hand trembled with the strain. My balance gave, the bird shot across the sink, and I landed flat against the refrigerator on the other side of the room. Two more attempts and I gave up and called Ali, who was relaxed in his leather chair listening to an old recording of the Koran being called out by a muezzin.

Ali obligingly freed the turkey of his entrails and I noticed that his hand also trembled as he dumped the bird in the sink. He went back to the Koran.

I went back to work on the beast, cleaning him inside and out. Now to the refill. Jeanne helped me with the wet sammoun concoction. We stuffed at both ends until he bulged indecently. We stitched him up, tied down his wings and legs. Then we stood back and observed. "Oh, isn't it horrid?" Jeanne shuddered as she said it, and in her sensitive presence I felt the whole procedure indeed vulgar. But it was done.

We covered the top surface of Jeanne's lacquered tray with aluminum foil, set the bird squarely in the center of it, lit a medium flame under the portable tin oven, and departed for the dining room, feeling somewhat proud of our stuffed accomplishment.

Only a few minutes passed and I heard Jeanne gasp, "Mrs. Baez, do look." I looked through the two screen doors and flames were leaping from the oven up to the cemented open chimney that luckily covered a quarter of the kitchen. Lizards, whose homes were secured in dark corners there, scrambled from their guard positions where they had been leisurely doing their push-ups, and disappeared up to cooler, untainted air.

Jeanne and I rushed to rescue Tom. We removed the tin portable oven with Tom in it over to the sink, trembling and dripping grease everywhere. The flames died down. Our

Thanksgiving dinner smelled like a burned-out paint shop. Poor old Tom looked sorely barbecued.

Try again. Clean out the burners, the oven, the tray. This time recover the entire tray and Tom himself. That done, Jeanne gingerly lit a match under the oven. We waited. She looked at me and smiled. Ali was quiet. "Is this Thanksgiving or the day of Holocaust?" I muttered, and we both laughed with nervous relief.

That fat beast sizzled and spluttered satisfactorily now. The lizards returned to their guard positions in the chimney and Jeanne and I got on with what we considered our "fat man's folly."

Our girls decorated the long table with eucalyptus pods and leaves and placed the white candles on the colored paper cutout doilies they had made.

Six hours later the puréed potatoes, creamed cauliflower, cranberry sauce, applesauce, pickles and olives—all tinned and bought at Spinney's store—as well as the hot sammoun, gravy, and the pièce de résistance, a slightly charred Tom Turkey, adorned the long dining table. The two families gathered. It was a picture from an old magazine of an American Thanksgiving.

Who was hungry? Nobody. Both husbands exclaimed about its beauty, heaped food on their plates, and nibbled. None of the children had appetites under normal circumstances, and Jeanne and I were both in a state of nauseous fatigue. Dinner was hardly touched when Ali brought in his surprise dessert. Its top glistened with a gluey, sweet-looking syrup. Under it was a soft, wet sort of a pudding. Because it was Ali and because it was a surprise, we did our best to show our pleasure with, "Oh Ali, you shouldn't have, really . . . " Then each of us cut a small triangle and faked a last shot of appetite. Luckily we had our paper napkins. Quite possibly we would have been more cooperative had it not been cooked with semne oil.

Relieved that the horrendous meal was over, the children left the table. The grown-ups slumped back and drank coffee, and in that quiet moment of relaxation I left the table, gathered our kids, and told them we had one more project to perform. It was one they enjoyed. We gathered as many paper plates as were left, about five and filled them with fruit, nuts, turkey, whatever we thought would be tasty to the children who daily gathered around the garbage pail looking for pomegranate seeds, bits of mildewed bread, meat, rice, anything, anything to fill some of those gnawing, empty holes inside. We stuffed the plates into paper bags, tied them with string, then stole out the back door, the iron gate, tiptoed to the tree that shaded the big pail where cats leapt out and scattered. We tied the precious bags to branches of the trees. We knew we were being watched, but we saw and heard nothing. We left quietly, ran upstairs, and watched out the bedroom window.

It was early evening. There was still a dusky glow in the sky. We could see only shadows. We heard the paper bags rustle, the thump of bare feet on the mud. Then silence. "Oh goody," came from one of the girls.

A ripple of giggles danced through the air. Even from our eldest who took to these Quakerly doings with a little less excitement than the other two. She too knew there would be some satisfied stomachs tonight. A happy sob escaped me when I heard the footsteps steal away.

Now to the grand clean-up. Jeanne had already started. There was Al with a dish towel on his arm. Even Ali peeked in on the women's work and chatted cheerily for a moment.

The girls had all conveniently disappeared. We didn't call them. It was so peaceful this way.

I teased Jeanne, who had hoped since she met Ali in England that they could live in the States, "How would you like to live in America and do this every year?"

She was quiet for a moment. So was the kitchen. We were all awaiting her answer. Then with her disarming smile and respectful voice, she answered, "Well, Mrs. Baez, it does complicate the decision somewhat."

The Movies and Our Bathroom—
The Best Shows in Town

Al

IT'S BEEN RAINING constantly for three days. We've been confined to our quarters in the house for the weekend and everyone is bored and restless.

"Let's go to a movie," says Mimi. "My friends at school tell me Abbott and Costello are playing at the Roxy."

"Oh, Popsy," says Joanie. "What a good idea! Shall we go?"

A glance around the room convinces me we've got a mandate. Abbott and Costello are not my favorite fare but under the circumstances even Pauline agrees it should be fun. Joan rings for a taxi. We scramble to find our rain gear.

It's been raining so long there's danger the Tigris will flood the lawns of the Semiramis Hotel. When we first arrived the river was almost twenty feet below the lawn level.

The movie houses are at the south end of the unpaved Ghazi Street. The taxi driver is flustered by our four good-looking females. "Don't worry, don't worry," he says to allay our fears as he slides on the muddy street, skidding slightly out of control every time he puts on the brakes.

The front of the theatre is mobbed by several hundred Iraqis who have our same idea. There is no such thing as a queue in

Baghdad. We have learned how to battle our way to the box office. For reasons of security and hygiene—lots of throat clearing and spitting going on—I buy a ticket for a box on the second floor where we can sit together. We can look down on the crowds as they scramble for seats and put their bicycles on the stage so they won't get stolen.

As if the human din were not enough, rain is falling on the tin roof above us and contributing several additional decibels of noise. Nothing dull about this place. It's a madhouse. As usual, the audience is predominantly male with the exception of a few Iraqi women in Western dress, probably wives of officials or high-level professionals who have lived abroad.

Suddenly a photograph of the king appears on the screen, the National Anthem blares out of the loudspeakers, and everyone stands. The sound system could probably win an Oscar for a combination of volume and distortion. No one seems to mind.

The house lights, which produce a greenish fluorescent glow, are only dimmed thus far because we will be treated to a fifteen-minute slide show of garish ads on the screen while vendors sell Coca-Cola and other goodies on the floor.

At last the theatre is darkened totally and the show begins with short segments of coming events. Marilyn Monroe's shapely and exposed body fills the screen, to the delight and howls of an exuberant male audience accustomed to seeing Baghdad women covered from head to foot. So much for Western cultural influence!

It's cold in this place! We huddle together for warmth. I sit Mimi on my lap. When the newsreel shows Anthony Eden the audience boos and a fight breaks out momentarily. Their rules for informal combat do not exclude kicking, which generates howls of pain. Things quiet down a bit although the rain on the tin roof keeps the background noise level about like that of a subway ride.

Finally Abbott and Costello come on and go through their antics. The film has a sound track in English and Arabic subtitles. I wish I could understand them.

But the movie does not run for very long. It has hardly

reached the halfway mark when it stops and the lights go on again for further sales of chewing gum, sandwiches, and Coke by vendors while more ads are projected on the screen. The excitement causes more clearing of throats, spitting, and men leaving for the bathroom. We are happy in the sanctuary of our box, munching on the date cubes and bananas we had brought along.

I can't remember a thing about the movie, but I do remember the nice feeling of being close to members of my family enjoying a respite from the normal routine of Baghdad life. Thank you, Thomas Edison, for inventing the movie projector. Soon the feature movie is over. We are subjected to the National Anthem once more, with people more or less standing at attention. Then a mad scramble for the bicycles on the stage and rivers of humanity oozing out of the exits. We stay in our box until the traffic has thinned out.

It has stopped raining but the street is muddy and slippery. It will be impossible to get a taxi for a while so we decide to window-shop. The street looks picturesque now that it's dark and the store windows are lit.

As we pass by a shop whose arched entrance is open I see something familiar and step inside, accompanied by my harem. It is a huge inverted cone of *halivah* about two feet high. The cone is about a foot wide and the flat top is about 6 inches in diameter. Elsewhere on the table there is an immense roll of what looks like shoe-leather.

"Good afternoon, sehr," says the shopkeeper. "What can I do for you today?"

"I am dying for some halivah and some *hamurdeen!*"

"Ah," he says, "you know their names and you pronounce them so well, like an Arab. Where did you learn about halivah and hamurdeen?"

"On Atlantic Avenue in Brooklyn," I say. "When I was a boy I lived just two blocks away from a Syrian neighborhood."

He laughs. "I have met Americans who knew about halivah but never before one who knew about hamurdeen!"

Actually, in Brooklyn we did call it "shoe-leather," but the shopkeeper there also taught me to say "hamurdeen." It is made from apricots and comes in sheets about three times as thick as brown wrapping paper. When I was a boy you could buy a large piece for a penny. It is absolutely delicious and has a mildly laxative effect if eaten in reasonable quantities. The difficulty lies in limiting your input to reasonable portions.

Halivah has the consistency of sawdust packed together with lard and you would never suspect that it tastes like heaven. But once you start eating halivah and hamurdeen, it's like salted peanuts—you simply cannot stop.

I have never seen a mountain of halivah as high as the one in this shop nor such large sheets of hamurdeen. The shopkeeper takes a huge knife and slices an immense chunk of halivah for me. He then rolls up what looks like a small sleeping-bag-sized portion of hamurdeen and off we go.

In the taxi on the way home I introduce my children to the sheer delight of these Middle Eastern savories whose appearance belies their delicious taste. By the time we reach the house we have made a noticeable dent in our supply. We feel like going back to stock up on these delicacies because it is clear they won't last long at this rate.

WHEN WE GET HOME from the movies there is a sudden demand for the bathroom facilities. These merit some description because they have interesting Middle Eastern quirks of their own. My women make a dash for the only western toilet in the bathroom downstairs. Necessity drives me upstairs.

Upstairs, in our quarters, there is an eastern style toilet—called Turkish in Baghdad—which consists of a hole in the floor at the edges of which are two slightly raised platforms about an inch high in the shape of crudely drawn feet. I dislike it because I'm not used to squatting and because, while using it, my nose is too close to the action. Flushing is accomplished by pouring water from a pitcher down the hole. At the college the Dean defended this design from a hygienic point of view by saying, "You don't have to sit where others have sat."

By comparison with anything in Baghdad, however, our

downstairs bathroom is superb and has more fixtures than most. A color photograph of it in a magazine would make it look elegant but it wouldn't tell you that ants come out from the drain in the floor, that you can get an electric shock by touching a clothes line in the room, or that loud vibrations set up in the plumbing sometimes persist for minutes and even hours without stopping—plenty of food for thought in elementary physics, chemistry, and biology!

Here is what is in the downstairs bathroom that serves four Kamals and five Baezes. There is a western-style toilet flushed by water from a huge cast iron tank near the ceiling with the words "THE GREAT NIAGRA" on it in raised letters as part of the casting. You activate it by pulling down the chain. A meek or slow pull won't work. It has to be a jerk with the right acceleration. When it *does* work you get a rush of water reminiscent of waterfalls followed by the loud trickle of water that fills the tank.

Then there is the old fashioned cast-iron bath tub covered with porcelain. The only trouble with ours is that it has a V-shaped bottom and it actually hurts to sit in it. It seems to have been designed with the intention of discouraging any of us to stay in it too long.

There is a shower that comes out of the wall. Its spray of water is not designed to enter the tub. It flows into a drain in the floor after hitting everything in the room, including the toilet. The floor gets soaking wet. Vile odors which defy Lysol come out of the drain hole.

The electric wiring is exposed and attached to the walls. Wet walls and floors make walking barefooted in the room a shocking and potentially lethal experience. I do not use an electric razor.

There is a bidet or sitz bath with many spigots and handles designed for women's hygienic needs but also useful for a quick lower body wash and even for rinsing clothes. Ours has more spigots than the ones in Paris—great for illustrating principles of hydrodynamics. One spigot shoots water straight up to the ceiling—quite a shock if you turn it on with your face too close.

The most colorful use made of this room occurs when the washerwoman comes to do our laundry. She is dressed in a black abayah. She has gold teeth, she knows no English, and she has had eight children, of whom four have survived. She squats on the floor, smokes cigarettes, throws her ashes all over the place, and tracks in mud from the outside when she goes out to hang up the clothes. She uses a flat circular pan about three feet in diameter and about eight inches high. She dumps the huge pile of clothes on the bathroom floor, takes one piece at a time, soaps it, scrubs it, wrings it, and puts it aside to be rinsed later. She pauses to take a puff on her cigarette and continues with her chore. When she finishes her cigarette she douses it in the rinse water and tosses it onto the wet floor and lights up another. Cigarettes doused this way produce a pungent odor that makes your eyeballs rock.

All in all, washday in Baghdad is a spectacle that cannot be matched in the U.S. In Baghdad just one look at the bathroom floor, littered with mud and cigarette butts, tells you it is wash day. It is a disaster but is also a theatrical event with the actress dressed in black, squatting and puffing away on a cigarette. This woman washes clothes for our entire family for 150 fils, or about 45 cents. We can't complain, therefore, about her smoking or the fact that she steals some of the clothing a few pieces at a time. Viewed as a real, live, off-Broadway production, washday is a bargain.

What Price a Hot Bath?

Joan

SOMEBODY WANTED A HOT BATH one morning, so I went to the back of the house with Al to light the water heater. I had never gone near any part of it. I was too frightened. I could do without hot baths forever. We could always heat pots of water on our safe three-burner kitchen kerosene stove.

This unusual invention crouched like a legless wide-backed animal outside, attached to the kitchen. It consisted of a cement kiln with openings in front and bricks on three sides, with a four-foot rail from the local train station cemented horizontally across the top of the front. A kerosene can sat on top and dripped slowly through a narrow pipe into the kiln when the spigot was turned on. The idea was to create enough vapor to keep a fire roaring to heat the water pipes that led to the giant drum beside the kiln.

Al opened the spigot and soaked some rags in kerosene, then tossed them into the kiln with a lighted match. I stood far back, my hands over my ears and face. When it didn't catch, I suggested that we heat a large vessel of water in the kitchen. Al didn't hear me. He threw in another match. He stepped back and waited. When it still didn't light he got impatient and turned the spigot so the kerosene would drip faster. I backed farther away. Fire never failed to freeze me with panic. I called to him in as controlled a voice as I could muster, "Please Abo, no more . . . it might blow!" But he was determined to make it work. "I'm too scared," I said, and ran into the house.

In the kitchen I got busy but my mind was outside with Al standing too near the explosive kiln. There had been many accidents all over Baghdad with these dangerous creations. Now, however, with his scientific curiosity, Al would make it work or find out why it didn't.

After about three minutes I heard a muffled, trembling explosion. I told myself it could be a door slamming or maybe the workmen had dropped a stack of lumber, all to ward off what my instincts told me was true.

Al appeared. His head down, eyes shut and his hands feeling for the door. He was stamping and moving his body as if he didn't know what to do with it. His hands and face and neck were charred, like rumpled charcoal. The front of his hair and his eyebrows were gone. His eyes—his eyes, I couldn't see them, and I was too frightened to think about them. He said in a near whisper, "I think I've been burned."

I told him to sit down and, because I had learned in some ancient first aid course that cool grease would soothe a burn, I began to pat oil and butter on his seared face and hands. Women from the neighborhood found their way to the kitchen where Al sat, and at the first sight of him they began wailing, holding their heads, calling in their friends, calling to Allah. They swayed back and forth. I looked desperately for someone who could help. Jeanne ran in. She chased the women out, then looked for someone who could understand that we needed a phone. "Please a phone, where is a phone?" She spoke first in English, then in some few words of Arabic.

A young student said to me, "Come, come." I left Jeanne with the oil and butter to soothe Al. The student led me to the phone where she called the American Hospital. She translated to me rapidly that we must take a taxi immediately and get down there. They would have a doctor ready.

The car arrived within minutes.

By now more hysterical women had flocked around. The taxi

driver, as nervous and excited as they, yelled *"Imshe—yella!"* and threatened to stone them. He helped Al into the car. He wired his claxon to a high, dissonant screech. Then his cab took wings.

We revved our way down the gutted road, through lanes and dusty drives, shooing goats, chickens, women, donkeys, and dogs in all directions. Al was in such pain that he could only stamp his feet and hit his elbows on his knees, twist his body, and say in a loud whisper, "Damn, damn!"

In twenty minutes we drew up to the hospital emergency entrance. The taxi man helped us through the door. I looked frantically for an attendant. To my great relief a quiet and soft-spoken Iraqi nurse appeared. She helped Al into a wheelchair and before saying a word, slipped a shot of morphine into his arm. She asked no questions until he was on the table in the faded green operating room. In minutes, Al's arms and legs and head stopped fighting. Only then did the nurse say to me, "Iss all right, Memsah. He rests a little now." Suddenly my feet felt the floor. She couldn't have known the depth of my simple thank you. She went on, "Only doctors give it morphine to patients, but this man, he has bery much pain, so I do not wait."

When the doctor arrived, he asked a few questions with an air of competence that immediately held my trust and started to work with the nurse, whose name was Amanda. They worked together for what seemed like a day and a night. I relaxed a little because Al was not in pain, while they cleaned his burns and wrapped him in bandages: hands, arms, chest, the entire head, leaving two holes in his face for his eyes, and a space for his mouth and nostrils. Only then did the caring Amanda leave. I knew she had stayed long after hours.

Al was already in bed in the dreary, dark green hospital room that smelled of ether and strong tobacco smoke when Ali walked in. With a commanding air he said to the doctor, "This man is to have the best in the hospital." He spoke some words of instruction in Arabic to the nurses and attendants. His voice was brittle, harsh. They answered nervously, "Na'am, Doctor, na'am. (Yes, Doctor, yes.)"

Ali then said to me, "You must come home with me. You cannot go home unaccompanied. It is too dangerous for a woman to travel by herself at night." Was it night already? I didn't want to leave Al alone.

I sat beside the bed for a short while after Ali left the room, staring into the holes in the bandages, watching to see if the eyes would open, and thinking about all that pain in there. An overwhelming feeling of sorrow and tenderness lowered over me like a heavy gray blanket. I wished he could know it. Then I kissed the thick bandage between the two dark holes, took a deep breath, and hoped that even in his sleep he could know my thoughts. I went out then to find Ali.

Two weeks later when we brought Al home in a taxi, it seemed as if the entire University was there. The students applauded and brought flowers and gifts, then asked, even pleaded, that they start classes immediately.

Al held classes in our bedroom for six weeks. His bandages were still on and the smell of burnt flesh, no matter how often the bandages were changed, was pungent and sour, but the students ignored it. They had to take buses from all over the city, then walk half a mile because we lived outside the city. They simply said, "Nevair mind, Doctor, we like it the classes."

Our three girls never complained about the "turble" smell; rather they were a lot more cooperative than usual about making the rooms look tidy, fixing the chairs for the students, and helping with the usual tiresome chores around the kitchen. Sometimes even Mimi, young as she was, joined us in picking the gravel out of the rice, cracking nuts, and setting the table for dinner or for the students. At that time, Joanie made up her own recipe for baking cake in our portable oven. The proportions were fine. She made a chocolate icing too. I thought it the best-tasting cake in Baghdad and made sure she served it to the students sometimes. I heard Pauline calling out often, "You okay, Pops?" I was as comforted as Al at all these attentions. I knew it was hard for the girls to see their father's bandaged head and hands.

The day came to take off the bandages. They had been

changed quite often, but I had never seen how well the burns were healing. Now I was afraid to see his face. I think I was as frightened as on that awful day of the accident, even though this time I knew he had his eyesight. How much pain would he have as they pulled away the gauze? Would his handsome face be scarred forever? Would his thick black hair be gone? I wondered if he had similar doubts.

The girls, solemn and a little nervous, waited in the drab waiting room at the hospital while I accompanied Al to the familiar green operating room. That sweet nurse, Amanda, first unbandaged his hands. They looked purple-red, oh so fragile. Then his head. I looked out the window. My knees didn't want to hold me up. Back again until his nose and chin, then his cheeks began to show. He was smiling with occasional twitches when the nurse touched a tender spot. The colors in his face were a mottled red, blue, and purple. The nurse said, "Nevair mind about the color, Memsah. It will soon be normal again." There was not a trace of eyebrow, but there were tiny stubbles, like early spring grass, where his hair had been burned off. I didn't mind; there was not a scar anywhere on his face, his head, or his hands, tender as they've been ever since. It seemed a miracle to me. I turned my back momentarily and thought a little prayer. I had to mop away a couple of persistent tears.

When the girls saw Al they didn't know quite what to say until Mimi broke out, "Oh Popsy! It's all better!" Al winked at me. It was truly all better.

Some days later, I ventured to the empty, burned brick wall behind the house where once the kiln had done its hazardous job of heating water. The workmen had disposed of the rubble that was left. There stood old Mahal leaning against the black wall. His gold teeth glittered in the sun. He was smoking the stump of a strong Turkish cigarette. "Memsah," he called pointing upstairs, "Sahib?"

"Yes, Mahal," I answered, "he's all better." I smiled at the concerned old man. Hard work and devotion were the roots of his life.

There was an almost raucous cheer everywhere in our house

the day Al returned to the University. That day Ali came to Al looking serious, but with a lifting of his forehead that made smile wrinkles. "My dear friend," he said, "do you think in the future that you could confine your experiments to the classroom?"

Al smiled and promised.

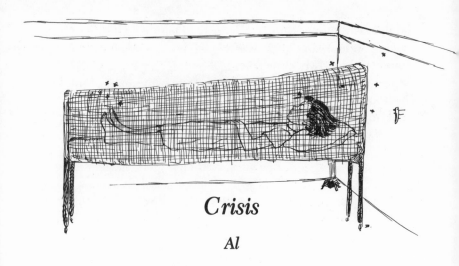

Crisis

Al

KNOWING SOMETHING ABOUT the low quality of medical care available in Baghdad, I kept hoping that nothing serious would happen to members of my family. I felt terribly responsible for having brought them to this difficult place full of dirt and disease. I was terrified that they might catch the so-called Baghdad boil which disfigured so many faces in this city.

The other thing that troubled me was that because my own work at the college was so demanding once teaching began I spent very little time at home. Joan bore the brunt of caring for the daily physical and human needs of the girls. The Baghdad experience was hardly a happy one for Joan.

One day, Joanie woke up with a nasty fever—aches and pains all over. She felt awful and Joan kept her in bed. Joan told me later that she had suspected, even in Paris, that Joanie had hepatitis because her skin had a yellow tinge. She hadn't dared to breathe this to any of us. Having been alone and so happy with Joanie in Paris, this had escaped my notice. But now Joanie, who had managed to evade hepatitis in California, when Mimi and Pauline had come down with it, succumbed to it in Baghdad.

We didn't even consult Ali. We just took Joanie to the American Hospital—Dar Al Salam—to see Dr. Piel. He was the only full-time doctor in the place. Part-time doctors came occasionally to help him during the week, but everyone else was an assistant without a medical degree. The young nurses who were being trained there were mostly from Baghdad, Beirut, and Mosul.

The American Hospital was, curiously, run by Seventh Day Adventists from Loma Linda, California, a town not far from our home town of Redlands. It was considered the best hospital in Baghdad, although it would not have met the standards of Loma Linda for want of facilities and trained personnel. I will, however, be forever grateful to the Seventh Day Adventists. In this hospital, part of the morning was devoted to a religious service in which the nurses participated. Joanie told us later that she could hear them singing in the distance.

Poor Doctor Piel was so overburdened with patients who were really close to death that, by comparison, a case of hepatitis must have seemed trivial to him. There were people in agony there, just barely able to stay alive, some of them looking like death warmed over. But, of course for us, Joanie was the most important. She was suffering and in need of attention. To Doctor Piel, Joanie was a patient who looked pale and thin but who could at least manage to get around on her own two feet, so he paid less attention to her than she deserved.

Shortly after having had a blood test, which made her weak, Joanie was sitting in the corridor when in walked two young women literally carrying an older woman who was absolutely rigid and looked dead. She showed no signs of life at all. They sat her down on the bench across from Joanie but she would flop over and the young women would have to prop her up again. One of them started to cry and Joanie, despite her own pain, felt sorry for the woman and said to Joan, "May I give her my candies?" Joan nodded yes, and weak little Joanie walked across the corridor and gave her candies to the melancholy woman, who smiled at Joanie.

Doctor Piel had not been able to make up his mind about Joanie's diagnosis and had made us come back on two previous occasions. But the ride to the hospital was so long, bumpy, hot, and tiring that on the third day we decided that Joanie should just stay there, no matter what.

So, when Doctor Piel passed by in the corridor Joan nabbed him and said, "Doctor Piel, I want you to look at Joanie's ankles: they are yellow! And look at her eyes: they are also yellow! Our other two daughters had hepatitis in California just before coming here. I'm sure Joanie has hepatitis!"

So Dr. Piel had to admit her to the hospital. An Iraqi medical attendant picked little skinny Joanie up in his arms and carried her upstairs to the ward. He deposited her on a recently vacated bed without even changing the sheets. Joan and I stayed in the hospital until it got dark. Our daughter finally went to sleep and we went back home feeling terrible. That night Joan wept.

Joanie stayed four days in the hospital. She told unbelievable tales of carelessness in hygiene. She was permitted to get into a recently vacated bed near the window, again, even before they had changed the sheets.

She came home to recuperate very slowly over a period of many weeks. One of the benefits of this interval was that she drew many sketches in a notebook which have helped us remember the incidents of life in Baghdad.

Those were trying times for all of us but especially for mother Joan, who grieved at the sight of her frail flower withering. Joan hated to see any of the girls suffer and it was pitiful to see Joanie, who had always been full of life, dragging herself around without any energy and not smiling with her accustomed spontaneity. The main ingredient of the cure was rest. In Redlands the doctor had told us the recovery would take at least six weeks, and that was with the help of drugs which were unavailable in Baghdad.

After about two months we sent her back to school. This was after Christmas. She came back full of pains. We attributed this to the long bumpy ride on the school bus so we tried using taxis. She still had trouble, so we took her out of school again until the end of the third quarter. By that time all three girls had had their fill of the Presentation School, so we took them all out of school. (In any case the fourth quarter would have run into July and we had planned to leave Baghdad by then because we had been told the heat would be unbearable.)

I marvel to this day that when I ask my children if they regretted the Baghdad experience Joanie, who suffered the most, says that in spite of everything she is not sorry we went. We all suffered in Baghdad, but, in spite of it, the experience enriched our lives in curious and subtle ways.

Me Chris, Memsah

Joan and Al

DECEMBER 15, AND THE AIR was beginning to smell like
Christmas. But in a Muslim country?

Yes, the American and British Embassies had already
imported their commercial symbols, evergreen trees from the
North, dress-up parties with lots of people, glittering decorations, and liquid fire.

The Catholic churches celebrated, of course. Theirs was a
solemn and religious celebration, perhaps more silent here than
in the Western countries. After all, the Christians were not the
chosen people in this land.

Even the janitors and servants had a new lift in their walk.
More than usual, we saw smiles and heard, "Me Chris, Memsah." It had to be Christmas.

Our family, too, would have Christmas in this Eastern land.
In the past the occasion had loomed large and exciting in our
lives. It would do so now. The fun of giving and receiving,
making and finding the special gift for each special person put
more punch into this season for us, we had to admit, than the
religious reason for it. However, we had always joined the
Quakers in some project to benefit a few who had no such
privilege as ours. There had been the Mitten Tree. We gathered
in friends who could knit. We handed out patterns, even put the

pattern in the local paper. Between the daily chores we knitted mittens of every design, shape and color. We bought a small tree and sometime during the vacation we had our party: soft drinks, home-made cookies, a bare tree that stood waiting for hundreds of pairs of mittens. When the party was over, the tree branches drooped low with mittens—enough to send great cartons of them to some cold and needy country.

This year we would do something in lieu of that project, but first we would make plans for a family Christmas. This year plans were especially necessary. We must stave off pangs of homesickness, that quiet and hopeless longing that unexpectedly, now and then, sent a teary face in search of a place to cry. A look, a photo, a name, especially on a card from a favorite friend. We were as vulnerable as rose petals.

The girls had already begun making things late in November after our disastrous Thanksgiving party. I saw the beginnings of tiny wool dolls, bracelets of pistachio nut shells, belts of watermelon pits, pin cushions. Pauline did the sewing, Joanie the drawing. I saw crayoned designs on plain materials, probably the beginning of bureau scarves and table mats. I found Mimi, now close to seven, knitting a doll's scarf. Treasures, all of them.

Our big treat was to visit Orosdibek's store on Rashid Street, the only department store in town. Like a skyscraper two stories high it stood among the rows of booths and cave-like shops that lined both sides of the street. A bright red neon sign announced its presence—"Orosdibek . . . flash flash . . . Orosdibek."

What a sight it was when we stepped off the bus. A giant Santa in full traditional red wool suit, scruffy white beard and grayish wig that sorely needed recycling, stood about twenty feet high. But he didn't stand still. He bobbled awkwardly forward as close to the window as his stretched pants would allow, then back, way back. We stood with the crowds outside, fascinated, laughing. He was so big, Oriental, and unlike any Santa we had imagined. Now and then there were hysterical screams from the children who weren't quite sure that he wouldn't break through the window and grab an armful of them.

We pushed our way through the doors. Neon lights blazed, unreal in Baghdad. Red and white crepe paper strung from wall to wall overhead, criss-crossed and twirled loosely, making the small bells tied to them bounce to eye-level. The counters were filled with flittering tinfoil pinwheels, handmade (in China) tiny cotton dolls with Oriental faces wearing hand-knitted dresses, pastel cotton balls, tinseled stars, celluloid angels, and all the members of the creche family filled compartments on the counters.

I kept hearing, "Get a load of this, Mom!" and "Did you check the bearded shepherds? They all came from China." Christmas symbols, all so ill-fitting in a Muslim city.

We stuffed our straw baskets with the unique ornaments. Now the questions was, where to hang them?

In the evening, one of the girls asked, "Pops, do you suppose we can have some kind of a tree?"

His answer, "Of course we'll have a tree." He put his brow-furrows together. They don't grow firs and pines in Baghdad. We could have one flown down from the north, or France, as the foreign clubs in town have done. That seemed so unimaginative.

"What about a palm-frond tree?" Al looked startled with his own brilliant idea. "A big one," he said, "and we can stick it in a big tub of sand. Then we can hang all those ornaments on it."

"Terrific!" I exclaimed, really taken with the idea.

"We can get popcorn and cranberries at Spinney's," Popsy said. "Jeanne did. We can string miles of them."

Not to be ignored, Mimi piped up, "And paper chains." We were on our way to having the most original tree in the Middle East.

The girls spent hours with the chain, coloring and cutting our paper designs to hang in the windows, small ones for the tree. We saved the tops and bottoms of tin cans, drew stars on them, then ruined the good scissors cutting them out. Mimi got the job of crayoning them. Joanie did the drawing and Pauline cut them. All these to make our magic tree.

The one joy of being in a foreign country at Christmastime was that all our friends remembered us. Each day Ali returned from the Arab bank where our mail was delivered, his arms laden with boxes and cards. "I think our American friends are going to start a department store in Baghdad," he said one day as he handed us another load of cards, packages, and letters of every color and size. We decorated the tile patio where we put the tree. We hung some cards on it—that crazy palm frond with the cotton balls, tinsel, pastel tin stars, celluloid angels and miles of popcorn and cranberry strings.

The girls wanted to go to a store to buy Baghdad presents. They wanted to have fun with their sparse allowances. We had heard of St. Joseph's Street where silverware was made. There they melted down Indian rupees and out of the silver they forged cups, bracelets, rings, trays, thimbles. We must see.

One day we put on our raincoats and boots, hired a taxi and drove off to St. Joseph's Street. The driver took us down Church Street where the Christian churches stood. Among others were the Latin Church, the Syrian, and the Greek Orthodox. All were solid, ancient stone buildings with ornate gold crosses and statues. We could see them through the fences and between the iron gates as we drove slowly through the mud where garbage floated on the running water on either side of us. The smell was pungent, but we held our breath automatically. We were used to it. The tidy small gardens, the green grass, the statues, the religion—everything seemed diametrically opposite to the sights and activity taking place only two blocks away on Rashid Street. We turned off and wound our muddy way to St. Joseph's Street.

There they were, the silversmith booths, a long line of small black caves, each one a factory where a turbaned man with long brown dress and bare feet sat on a stone or wooden bench and worked at his forge against the black wall. The flames roared high, died down, and went high again. Looking closer we could see that under each forge was a young boy, sometimes no older than seven or so, who hand-pumped bellows that shot the flames high when he was signaled by his master's rasping shout.

The workmen stopped now and then to greet us. Their faces looked like aging leather. They smiled. "Memsah wish to see?" one of them asked me. The little boy crawled out from his squatting position below the forge. He stared at us while his boss, probably his father, pointed out the handiwork in his glass-covered showcase—handmade silver on black velvet. Every item was a shining work of art. How many hundreds of years have these people engraved or enameled these same designs onto every article, I wondered. I had seen them on wooden souvenirs, baskets, on nearly everything that needed a design. There were scenes from the Tigris River, fishermen whirling down it with their *goofas* (round, basket-like boats), the great arch of Ctesiphon that we had visited, a mosque with a minaret, a palm tree by the river, camels with their masters, and many, many more, carefully and accurately copied from life. We asked where the designs came from, but no one knew their history or date, only that they were hundreds of years old.

After looking at the various booths, we split up, with the agreement that we'd meet at this big mud-hole where we were standing. Joanie and Mimi wandered in one direction, Pauline and I in another, and Popsy meandered between us within ear-shot for bargaining when the time came. He had become as adept at it as a native, except that rather than having a heated argument and kicking the merchant, he ended up with a handshake plus what he thought was a good bargain.

I loved the shopping, the street scenes, and the people; but I dreaded showing any of my loot to Ali, because he had to tell us each time that we must learn to shop. He summoned up his teaching voice and preached to us the lesson that we never learned.

"Let me see what you have bought," he said jovially the day we brought home our precious silver. Reluctantly I unwrapped a ring and what I thought a beautiful bracelet for one of the girls.

"Ah," Ali said. "This is very nice. What did you pay for it?" I laughed at the question because I had expected it. Then I told him.

His face changed from teasing good humor to frowning annoyance. "My dear," he said, "this is foolish. You have paid far too much."

I had a great desire to say,"Oh, shut up," but I waited for the rest of his speech.

"How do you expect to gain the respect of those merchants in the zucs if you let them get away with this sort of thing?"

"Horrors," I said, feeling annoyed, "what's that got to do with it? You know what I think, Ali?" Now I was taking my life in my hands. "The extra fils mean a whole lot more to that fellow and his family than their respect does to me, so I'm perfectly happy to pay for it."

By Christmas Eve our palm frond tree stood in its sand tub wrapped with red crepe paper in the small tiled patio. The two Kamal children, Susan and Gay-Gay, had joined our girls in making the decorations. Now every branch was heavy with the creative efforts of all of them.

Too tempted to hold out, one of the girls asked, "Can't we open just one package now?"

"How about just one each," I said. Suddenly I was popular. Actually I was as anxious as they were. The familiar labels and boxes were as exciting to us as a new shiny truck would be to a little boy. Grapenuts never looked so crunchy, nor Hershey bars so rich and chocolatey. We passed the bar around and smelled it. Some good friend had made raspberry and strawberry jam. Aha, was that golden brown jar really my own favorite? Yes, somebody back home was endowed with second sight. There was a large jar of nutty grind peanut butter. God was surely in His heaven!

Christmas Eve in Baghdad. Close to midnight, the sound of a taxi horn broke the cold silence of the night. Joan and I put on winter coats, took a last look at the sleeping children and locked the house gate behind us.

Fuad, the taxi driver, took us across the Tigris to the English church by a roundabout route because there had been a fire on Rashid Street. We commented on the beautiful Pontiac he was driving. The Pontiac belonged to Najim, who owned a fleet of good cars and catered to the foreign personnel at the embassies. Fuad lamented that his own salary of 15 dinars a month would never permit him to own a taxi. Yet Fuad was better off than Hamid the policeman, who got only seven dinars a month and had five children—boys, that is—he didn't count his two girls.

The night was so cold that a white vapor puffed out of the exhaust pipe as the taxi idled in front of St. George's Episcopal Church.

"Will you call back for us, Fuad?"

"I come back in an hour, Doctor."

Inside the cold church a wheezy organ had just finished playing a hymn which the scattered congregation had sung without animation. The venerable archdeacon Claude Roberts conducted the service in a mournful tone. The Aladdin kerosene stoves, used universally in Baghdad for heating, lined the edges of the center aisle. In the dimly lit church the bluish flames at the bottom of the evenly spaced stoves added a pleasant visual touch to the scene. But even ten stoves going full blast were not enough to heat this dreary old stone church on such a cold night.

A funereal air pervaded the temple. The smell of the kerosene vapor overpowered that of the incense. The hymns were sung in a perfunctory and dirge-like manner. Where, oh where, I asked myself, is the warmth of Christmas at home in Redlands, with carols and the gayly lit tree? Or the voices of Puerto Rican children singing carols in Spanish in my father's church in Brooklyn?

Members of the British and American embassies were present, all wearing overcoats. There was also a truckload of soldiers from the British base at Habbaniya. The service was over none too soon for us and we headed for the door. We all shook the archdeacon's hand mechanically as we left.

"This way, Doctor," said Fuad, holding open the taxi door for us.

"Thank you, Fuad. Please take us home by way of Rashid Street if you think it has been cleared after the fire."

We took the King Faisal Bridge across the Tigris to Rashid Street instead of following our usual route across the railroad bridge near Al Waziria. The fire on Rashid Street had been put out, but water and debris covered the street and we skidded along on a gooey mess for several blocks. Before long we were driving on dry pavement.

Baghdad had never been so quiet. The dogs must have been frozen in their tracks. It was too late for traffic on Rashid Street. It was like driving down a long black corridor. It seemed strange to pass by familiar entrances to bazaars which were now oddly devoid of people and noise. They looked like black empty caverns. I wondered what went on inside these endless labyrinths at this hour of the night?

Even at the normally bustling intersections—called circuses —there was a strange silence. Only an occasional gasoline lantern illuminated the beat of a lonely policeman.

We bid Fuad farewell with *"Fi aman el lah."*

Fuad said, "Fi aman el lah," and then, "Ashkurak," as I pressed a dinar into his hand. He smiled and tilting his head he gave me a weak imitation of a military-style salute.

After the taxi left we could see a few stars through the fleeting windows to the sky produced by clouds rushing by, but it was too cold to stay out and watch. It was very late. Not even Mahal came to the iron gate. We had told him we would use our own keys to enter the *mushtamel*, the servants' quarters which had become our apartment.

We passed through the little dining room decorated for the occasion with a palm branch for a Christmas tree on which we'd hung home-made cotton balls and trinkets. A tin-foil star made from chewing gum wrappers listed unsteadily at the top. Christmas cards from friends back home dotted the wall. A few presents were scattered round at the foot of the wooden box that served as a tree stand.

Joan and I were tired and ready for sleep, but Joan would rather die than go to bed on Christmas Eve without filling the stockings for which she had prepared in secret for many nights after the children had gone to bed. I have always been a weary and reluctant helper in this ritual but never the engineer. This is Joan's department.

Joan fixed a cup of hot tea and, thus fortified, we began putting trinkets into the children's stockings. Pauline was thirteen, in that never-never land between childhood and womanhood, but Joan fixed a stocking for her as well. Joan had performed miracles in finding baubles at the bazaars and the Indian stores. I could hardly keep my eyes open. I cheated by stuffing oranges into the stockings—a cheap way to fill up space. They were bulky, plentiful, and very good in Baghdad around Christmas.

As I stuffed the stockings I couldn't help comparing Christmas in Baghdad with last year's Christmas in Redlands. Uncle George and Auntie Barbara had come all the way from Laguna early in the morning loaded with presents for everyone. My brother Peter had come from Montana and my nephew Skipper had come from San Francisco. We had gathered round a huge Christmas tree loaded with tinsel and bright lights. There had been dolls for Mimi, a newly painted second-hand bicycle for Joanie, a plaid bathrobe for Pauline, a new record player for Joan and me. There had been something for and from everyone in the house. Extra leaves had been put into the old oak table until it had filled the dining room area. We had a wonderful chicken dinner, slavishly and lovingly prepared by Joan. We had had silent grace after the manner of Friends before the meal. We had reminisced and sung and played and had been bound by the mysterious halo of warmth and friendship which only Christmas can bring. By comparison the Baghdad setting was meager and sad.

With such thoughts of Christmas past I now took a last look at the sleeping children. On such occasions I always wondered if I'd done wrong in bringing them to Baghdad where they were deprived of the simple joys to which they were entitled and which they had had back home. I crept into bed and lay awake pondering our situation and finally fell asleep.

No sooner had I closed my eyes, it seemed, than the chanting of the Koran from a distant mosque awoke me. This meant it was four o'clock in the morning on Christmas day.

"There is no God but Allah and Mohammed is his prophet . . . "

It was Christ's birthday but it had begun with a chant inspired by Mohammed. Not that Mohammed would have denied a share of glory to Christ, whom he acknowledged as one of a long line of prophets. But somehow I couldn't make the Koran blend in my mind with "Hark the herald angels sing . . . "

Only minutes later, it seemed, it was 6 A.M. and the children dashed down to the dining room where we had hung the stockings. Joan and I had hoped they would sleep late or at least entertain themselves quietly with their stockings. Not a chance! Part of the fun was to bring the presents to our bedroom where they sat on our bed and pulled the trinkets and oranges out of their stockings. We laughed together about the trinkets and how inadequate they seemed for the occasion. We all sensed that this was a sort of make-believe Christmas. If there was sadness it was glossed over by laughter and a warm family feeling.

We had breakfast together in the crowded little dining room where the palm branch served as a Christmas tree. Now all the other presents could be opened. Susan and Gay Kamal swelled the volume of childish laughter in the crowded room. They also had presents under the tree.

I surprised the family by playing Christmas tunes I had tape-recorded from an album at the USIS. Familiar Christian hymns and carols filled the house of the Muslim Ali Kamal. We tried singing but something was missing. We couldn't get into the spirit of it.

The children were immersed in a sea of noise and laughter for which the music was only a background, but Joan sat and listened to it quietly in a corner. She lowered her head as if meditating. The music of Handel and Bach were transporting her in space and time.

A long silent interval on the tape caught all of us off guard and forced us to be quiet. Then Bach's "Joy of Man's Desiring" began to play. Joan reached for a handkerchief. After listening to a few bars of this piece she walked to the door shaking her head and wiping her eyes. We listened to the rest of the piece in silence. A wave of nostalgia and sadness had broken over all of us.

At this point Ali and Jeanne came in to pay their respects. This provided a welcome change in scene. Ali wanted to repeat his invitation to have us join the Kamals for Christmas dinner. Ali was culturally a Muslim but he was not religious. He had studied in England, married an English woman, and enjoyed Christmas festivities which he associated with pleasant times in England.

Meanwhile, on the tiled floor veranda at the back of the house, Mahal, our factotum, was gayly plucking feathers from a turkey he had recently strangled. In the back yard he had dunked the bird in a huge pot of boiling water. The path from the back yard to the kitchen was strewn with turkey blood. Mahal had killed the bird by wringing its neck and had walked into the kitchen in search of a pot holding the inverted bleeding bird upside down by its legs. I can still see that macabre grin of his. This was *his* gobbler. He had fattened it up and kept it in a special mud hut which he had built with the same technique used by the natives to build their living quarters. When wet, the earth in Baghdad works like clay and dries into bricks in the sun.

At dinner papa Ali was host, chief carver, Sheik, and master of all masters. He lit some candles which he had kept hidden in a beautiful box made of inlaid wood from Damascus. He generously served us the choice cuts of turkey. Jeanne and Joan had done the cooking but Ali, as head of the household, did the honors and served with a flair and a flourish.

OUR FAMILY HAD ONE more thing to do; just as at Thanksgiving, we had filled baskets for whoever was outside the gate. This time the baskets were prettier, with Christmas trimming of red and green crepe paper, pomegranates and other fruits, ribbon candy, lots of pistachio nuts, Christmas cookies, and tinsel over everything.

As we got over the front door, we heard up and down the road, "Memsah, me Chris." It seemed as if the whole town of Al Waziria was Christian and standing outside our gate and down the road. They had learned Joanie's name, "Choanie, me Chris." Joanie emptied her basket and pockets within minutes. So did we all, and on all sides we heard, "Askurich, Memsah, askurich." Some folded their hands and bowed their heads as they thanked us. When the baskets were empty we headed for home, only about a block away. Mimi and Joanie skipped and pirouetted in circles. The Arab children, even the little girls, laughed. That was the good sound of Christmas—children laughing.

This time next year, I thought, we'll all be home, remembering this day on the dusty road. Maybe we wouldn't even believe it had all happened.

At the end of the long day, Jeanne and I sat on the back porch. There was a dusky pink light in the sky. We had a cup of tea in our hands and we spoke of Christmas at home. I knew she was dreadfully homesick. She breathed a long sigh, close to a sob. "Oh dear," she said, "I wonder how my mother and father are getting along." Her head was down and I heard tears in her voice, but she looked up abruptly as if to shake off her sadness. "Do you think the children had a good time, Mrs. Baez? I do hope so."

I searched for words that might comfort her, but found none. "I know they did, Jeanne. You know why? Nobody fought all day."

"Oh," she laughed lightly. "Truly?"

I raised my teacup. "Let's drink to Christmas in a Muslem city—this time a holiday with no disasters."

WE ALL LOUNGED IN THE huge Kamal living room and listened to more recorded music. The sleepy period which follows a long day of eating and resting soon set in and we retired to our respective quarters with many good wishes and salaams.

Before we knew it it was getting dark again. The girls were exhausted and went to bed early. Joan and I didn't last much longer. Sitting up in bed we reviewed the events of this strange Christmas day. We exchanged comments until Joan fell asleep.

I was restless and got up. I walked out onto the big roof patio. This afforded me a clear view of the outskirts of the city in all directions. The night had turned cool and clear. The stars were brighter than usual. I recognized the sound of a bell from one of the distant Christian churches huddled together near the center of Baghdad.

Only a block away, facing east, on the raised dyke that protects Baghdad from the floods of the Tigris, I could see, silhouetted in the moonlight, a lonely shepherd leading a long line of sheep whose hooves had raised a cloud of dust. I could hear the rumble of the earth produced by their jog-like steps and the occasional *baa* of the sheep. And on this clear cool night, under a canopy of stars in a Muslim land, I imagined that shepherds watched their flocks by night and wise men rode to do homage to the Christ child.

The Group Photograph

Al

Dean Duri posted an announcement saying that a group photograph of the students and faculty of the College of Arts and Sciences would be taken by a professional photographer on the steps of the nearby School of Medicine, an easy twenty-minute walk from our college. This place was chosen because it was big enough to hold all 150 students and the 30 members of the faculty. It would take place a week from Wednesday at ten o'clock in the morning.

I was delighted at this opportunity to take a photograph of the entire student body and faculty. My Voigtlander Vito 35mm camera was small enough to tuck into my shirt pocket when folded, and I carried it with me most of the time to shoot pictures which someday would become a slide and tape show.

Hassan Ahmed Hassan showed up at my office at 9:30 on the appointed day. "Good morning, Professor Baez," said Hassan. "I'm here to guide you to the School of Medicine. But it's much too early. You'll see, no one will come on time."

We left the office and started to walk toward the designated place. "I'd rather get there early than late, Hassan," I said. "Besides, it will give me time to chat informally with students and with teachers outside my department whom I seldom get to see."

We arrived at 9:40 and there was not a soul in sight. At 10:00, the appointed time, there were only two other people besides

Hassan and me. They were the other members of my Unesco team. No sign yet of the Dean or the photographer. People ambled in slowly. A holiday mood prevailed. No one seemed pressed for time.

My students were among the first to arrive. I was introduced to faculty members from other departments. By 11:00 almost everyone was there but still no sign of the photographer or the Dean. It seems that people show up in inverse order of their importance on such occasions. People gravitated to the places which seemed natural: students stood up in the rear steps and faculty members sat down in the front rows.

At last the photographer lumbered in carrying the largest view camera I've ever seen. It seemed vintage 1850. The students applauded. They were in a festive mood. An assistant brought along a huge wooden tripod which he began to assemble. Together the photographer and his assistant lifted the monstrous camera to the top of the tripod and secured it. It was now about eight feet above the ground and the photographer had to climb a ladder to view the image on the groundglass screen, covering both his head and the camera with a black cloth.

Now Dean Duri arrived and was greeted with applause. He was on stage, so to speak, and the audience was ready for the play to begin. But the photographer was still not ready. The assistant had to go and fetch the photographic plates which were at least five by seven inches in size.

While the photographer continued to fidget I ran out in front of the crowd, determined to take advantage of this unique photo opportunity. This unheard-of and undignified behavior on the part of a professor enhanced the air of merriment. I knew I could take at least three shots before the professional even got the first plate into his camera. From previous experience I knew I could make everybody laugh simply by saying, "one, two, three" in Arabic. It was my mispronunciation that brought the house down: "*Wahed, thnein, thelathe!*" The effect exceeded my wildest expectations. It caused the Dean to toss his head back and let out what could only be called a whoop.

Decorum had been tossed to the winds all because this crazy American professor had broken the rules.

As soon as the professional had finished taking pictures, which took at least another fifteen minutes, I took my film downtown to have it processed. They knew me in the shop and promised to have prints ready the next day.

I suspected it would take several weeks before proofs came back from the professional, so I passed around copies of my prints to people who were close to me like Hassan and Shauki. I asked them to make a list of people who wanted copies.

But, unfortunately, one of the prints reached Dean Duri. It was the one in which he had been caught in the undignified position, laughing with gusto, his head tossed back with abandon. He called me into his office.

"Professor Baez, I admire your photographic skills, but you must not distribute copies of the photograph you took. We have hired a professional photographer and it would undermine his business." That was how he began but he went on to explain that a photograph which reflected poorly on the dignity of the faculty would reach people outside our circle of college friends. It would do damage to his cause and weaken support from the Minister of Education.

I had much to learn about protocol and proper behavior patterns. On a previous occasion I had suggested that I could save time by riding a bicycle instead of walking and taking taxis but Dean Duri had begged me not to do so. "It is most undignified. No professor would ride a bicycle in Baghdad. People would ridicule not only you, the Unesco-appointed professor, but me as well, because I condoned such undignified behavior. Besides, it is very dangerous. People driving cars in Baghdad have been known to knock down cyclists and then run away."

I recalled my prints as Dean Duri had asked. But I kept a copy, and have saved it in an album all these years. Whenever I look at it I am reminded of the Baghdad days. I don't think it will hurt anyone to see it now, thirty-seven years later; even Dean Duri would laugh all over again!

Friday Afternoons

Al

IT IS FRIDAY. There is no school today. Good Muslims go to the mosque. Others sit in tea houses smoking a hubble-bubble, playing checkers, or twirling prayer beads, and, mostly, talking.

The door bell rings at our house in Al Waziria. Mimi goes to the door and lets Naseeb in. Mimi, who is only six, likes Naseeb because he has an aristocratic air and is tall and good looking. She is about half as tall as he. She looks very cute in her bangs and boyish bob of dark hair which contrasts pleasantly with her greenish eyes. She holds his hand as they walk to the stairs leading to the mushtamel.

Naseeb arranges chairs in a circle in our living room in preparation for the meeting of silent meditation which we have been holding on Fridays as an experiment in non-exclusive worship. He sets copies of the Koran, the Bible, the Book of Mormon, and the Bhagavad Gita, all in English translation, on a side table. Our idea is that anyone can pick up one of these holy books during the silences and read from it, either silently or aloud, if he feels moved to do so. Only once or twice has anyone actually tried it, but it is appreciated as a symbol of ecumenism.

Today two of my students, Sadiq Fadhil and Suad Al-Ali, attend out of curiosity. We sit in a circle. Mimi sits near Naseeb.

Before long Joan, Joanie and Pauline join us. Some of us close our eyes as we meditate; others bow their heads with eyes open or shut. The procedure is patterned after the manner of worship followed by the Quakers (Religious Society of Friends), but we don't call it a Quaker meeting. The basic idea is to sit in silence in an attitude of receptiveness to the Spirit of God.

After about half an hour, Joan, Pauline, and Joanie leave the room to fix tea. Mimi remains near Naseeb. The girls are probably happy to have a legitimate excuse to leave early. They have never openly rebelled against attending Friends meetings but they were highly critical of some older Quakers in the Redlands Meeting whom they considered sanctimonious.

Now we hear them approaching the door, so I take the initiative to end the silence by extending my hands to my neighbors. We all do the same and hold hands in a circle for a few seconds. This terminates the silence and we are all served tea and biscuits.

And now we chat informally, taking this opportunity to meet the students and learn how they have come, out of interest, to see what silence worship is like. Silence has a mystical way of opening up communication at a deeper level than you usually find in the chit-chat of a cocktail party.

Our earlier attempts at silent worship in Baghdad had been abortive. Alan Peters, an English Quaker who had corresponded with me before coming to Baghdad had written, with a hint of missionary zeal uncharacteristic of Quakers: "There is much to do in Baghdad, Albert." He had invited members of the faculty to meet in the sumptuous home of a wealthy Iraqi woman, Madam Jamali, on the banks of the Tigris in the north of the city. These meetings failed because their purpose had not been made clear. Madam Jamali associated sitting quietly around in a circle with spiritualism and "table tipping," and she became impatient with the long periods of silence. The professors, not knowing that group silence was one of our objectives, once used a meeting as a forum to air their political views. One very anti-American British professor married to an Iraqi woman railed against American support for the Jews, who he said "had made the desert bloom but had obtained the land through immoral actions." The Swiss professor wanted to tell us about his participation in the Moral Rearmament Movement. Once, when we held a meeting during a picnic in the desert by the banks of the Tigris, the Pole was more interested in picking samples of the flora of Iraq than in "waiting in silence upon the Lord."

Eventually, though, we started our Friday afternoon gatherings and invited students and friends instead of just college faculty members. The weekly affairs became a success.

An important by-product of these meetings was that Naseeb Dajani became a life-long friend. He had attended Catholic schools in Palestine and had great respect for some of his teachers there. He was also on good terms with Father Connell of the Baghdad College. Nevertheless, he was a dedicated Muslim who gave me my first insight into what that can mean.

He once brought his mother to the meeting. She was a cultured, articulate, and dignified Arab woman. I met no other such woman in Baghdad. Baghdadi women were very conservative. They were not supposed to have informal social contacts with men. In the street all Arab women in Baghdad wore the black abayah which covered them from head to toe. Mrs. Dajani did not. She and the women students at the college, once they were within its gates, were among the few Arab women I saw in Baghdad without the veil.

We never met Naseeb's father, but Naseeb told us that he was a teacher and a religious leader. Naseeb's attitudes and behavior showed the influence of strong, educated, and devout parents. They were Palestinians who had fled their home country during the Arab-Israeli war.

The Dajanis were an aristocratic family, as was apparent from Naseeb's bearing and speech. In speaking to my girls Naseeb often said that the Dajanis were "the best in all Palestine," which he pronounced "Palesteen" prompting Joanie to imitate him and repeat, with an impeccable British accent, laced with a tinge of Arabic in which the R's are slightly rolled:

"We Dajanis are the best in all Pales*teen*." It became a family joke and the girls always repeated it when Naseeb came to visit.

Another consequence of these Friday gatherings was that they set a pattern for similar meetings we would hold with students when we returned to Redlands. In fact, what we learned from our experiments with community silence, in a world where finding the time and the place to be quiet in the presence of others has become increasingly difficult, may be among the most valuable treasures we brought home from our year in Baghdad.

It is now Friday evening. Joan is preparing toast on which we will, as usual, spread some jam. Pauline says to Joanie, "Which of the students did you like best—Suad or Sadiq?"

Joanie says, "I liked Suad because he had curly hair but I can't understand why he wears a bow tie."

Mimi chimes in, "I still like Naseeb best."

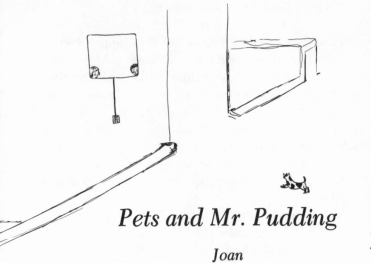

Pets and Mr. Pudding

Joan

THE MAN WHO LIVED ACROSS the street was a Captain in the Army. He was fat, *very* fat. We called him Mr. Pudding. We often saw him late in the mornings in his white pajamas, strutting pompously about on the roof and on his grounds. As a captain surveys his ship and the vast sea around him, so Mr. Pudding eyed his grassless lawn, his withered geraniums, and his chimney, whose stones were visibly crumbling. Sometimes he summoned his gatekeeper to open the gate and he ventured a few yards down the road, looking important.

He liked children, especially ours, because he could try out his English on them. He told them he was a lover of animals and all birds. "You like it birds?" he asked Mimi one day, and Mimi nodded. "Iss good, I shall bring it for you a surprise tomorrow in the afternoon, izzent-it?"

Mimi said, "That's nice," and ran into the house to tell me.

The next afternoon Mr. Pudding arrived at the gate with a large cage in his hand and all three girls ran out to greet him. I watched at the window and beckoned to Jeanne to watch with me. "What is it?" she asked, as curious as I. Her two little girls stood by the door hugging their dolls and looking shy.

Pauline, Joanie, and Mimi looked eager and bounced around at first. They peeked in the cage and then there was a decided change. No more bouncing and no more smiles, rather a look of horror, then anger. Pauline came in. "What is it, Pauline?" I asked, and she who seldom showed us a teary face, squeezed her eyes and lips tight for a moment. Then, while tears rolled down her cheeks, she choked, "That stupid, dumb Mr. Pudding brought two pretty white doves, but they can never fly because he clipped their wings. Oh . . . !" she turned to the door and ran upstairs.

Joanie marched in next, her face black with fury. "Did Pauline tell you? Pretty white doves and they'll never fly." Mimi was behind her and well caught up in sympathy for the birds and anger at the pompous Captain who thought he was being kind.

I ran out to thank him and ask him how to care for the birds, what to feed them, and where to shelter them. "Yes, Memsah," he announced, to the surrounding fields and mud huts, "I make it nice pets for your children, izzent-it?" and he turned to Mahal, whose bloodshot eyes missed nothing. Mr. Pudding shouted something in Arabic to him. Mahal padded over and took the bird cage, carried it upstairs to the roof, and built a shelter of wood slats. Pauline brought some dry weeds and Joanie and Mimi brought water and bread, but the birds huddled, a fluttering duo at the back of their new shelter.

We left the roof with misgivings about their stick-like delicate feet touching the searing tile roof. "They can't even fly to the scrub trees," Joanie complained woefully.

Early the next morning while I was heating water for our ersatz coffee, Mahal arrived with one of the precious birds in his gentle brown hand. "Memsah," he called. I was startled when he showed me the holes where the eyes had been. He explained in gestures that a night bird had plucked out the eyes of both birds. He motioned to me to follow him to the roof. There was the other frightened creature, his wings hanging. He was trying valiantly to hop somewhere, anywhere, but if we had left him, Mahal motioned that he'd plummet to the ground as the other one had because he was blind. I was horrified, shaky.

"Please, Mahal, take it away," I motioned. "It's so miserable."

Mahal, who often had a devil's gleam in his eyes possibly dreaming of fried pigeon for dinner, picked up the trembling bird and tucked it with the other in his arm. "Aye, Memsah, aye," he said, and he carried them both away.

Nobody spoke that morning at breakfast. I tried cheering the girls with my own belief that the birds would never have to struggle again. "No more clipped wings and hot roofs," I ventured, "and nobody knows but I think that maybe birds have their own heaven where they can fly forever." My response was silence and an occasional muffled sigh.

"How come Mr. Pudding says he loves his dog, then kicks him and makes him scream like a baby?" Mimi asked one morning. She had seen it happen. So had I. The emaciated old dog had yelped truly like a child all the way across the yard.

"I don't know, Mimi," I said, feeling anger up to my throat. "Their way with animals here is just different, and I guess we can't change it." She got a better answer from Ali later when she asked him. He saw that she was distressed and he knelt down to her level. "My dear," he said, "these dogs are wild and vicious. They're part jackal and they come in from the desert. These people keep them to guard their houses. They are not pets. They are frightened and hungry and full of diseases. You must never touch one of them." Ali said that they learned in the Koran when they were children that dogs were unclean, "and we are never to touch them. Remember that."

Mimi held back her anger and she looked away. "I hate Mr. Pudding," she said.

Two days later Joanie rushed in from the road. "Mum, he's dead, Mr. Pudding's dog is dead," she choked. I followed her out and yes, poor old Ramah, the big brown female, lay in the gutter as if peacefully sleeping. Her head was still bleeding. Joanie ran into the house and just then Mr. Pudding strode out, "She is crying, your daughter?"

"Yes," I said. "She can't understand why your dog is dead. Did somebody shoot her?"

"It was bedy bad," he said, looking not one bit convincing. "I love it my dog Ramah, but she was bedy bad. Always she is biting my maid in the feet when she is coming to work in the mornings. So I have to shoot it the dog. I will get it another, Madame, I love it my dogs."

True to his word, Mr. Pudding showed up some days later with a small, mangy mongrel named Findik that barked nervously in high sharp yelps perpetually. It was at night that we finally had to ask Mr. Pudding if he could quiet his dog. "Yes sair, Doctor, he will be quiet tonight." In panic I said to Al, "He'll probably shoot this one, too," and I was actually relieved to hear Findik start his nocturnal vigil as soon as the sky darkened.

Not Al. He said, "I'll fix that guy," and his inventive mind began to spin. He had brought his somewhat primitive tape recorder from the States. He plugged it in and hung the microphone out the window. There we all were, crouched below it. When Al had some good footage of doggie bark, he put the loudspeaker up to the window and turned up the volume. Now we had the dog plus his recording going together. Lights turned on in the house across the street, first upstairs, then down and finally outside. We made ourselves invisible behind the curtain. Now Findik stopped momentarily, sat on his haunches, pricked up his ears and leaned forward like the Victrola dog listening to "His Master's Voice." Mr. Pudding saw him and he looked confused. We had a hard time keeping from laughing. Mr. Pudding called then, "Choanie, Choanie, I think you make it tricks." Little did he know that it was Choanie's father who was making it tricks. We remained silent. Their lights went out. Everything was quiet, oh so quiet. We pussy-footed back to bed laughing and whispering and Findik started to bark once again.

Mr. Pudding's pet became Joanie's pet. One day she saw the poor hungry little mutt, all rib bones, skinny legs, and a rat tail that formed a crescent between his hind legs. He had retrieved a banana peel from the garbage pail and was chewing at it savagely. Joanie was all tears and sobs when I found her on the porch. "I don't care what silly old Ali says, that poor little dog is starving and I'm going to feed him." She marched off to the kitchen and I didn't stop her.

I heard her, "Come on, Findik, come here doggie," as she called from behind the door. The dog had seen the dish of corn flakes and milk and started to creep up to it like a frightened baby fox. He was just about that size, and too scared to touch the dish, but too hungry not to. I froze to my cushion. Findik slunk out and had his fill. We watched his tummy expand just as the ticks did on his back.

Two days later Jeanne and her two little girls stood in awe when they saw Joanie holding Findik lightly with one arm while she carefully twisted off the ticks from his body and methodically drowned them in a bowl of water. "One, two, three . . . " and a wonderful child laugh with every count.

Joanie had completely won Mr. Pudding's pet. Findik sat on the dry mud in the road and waited to see her come home from school. His nose quivered and his ears stood up like artichoke leaves. When she appeared she called him and he ran so fast he almost turned head over heels to get to her. My greatest joy was to see his tail not just wagging, but spinning like a windmill.

One day Mr. Pudding was watching. "You touch it dogs?" he asked her, looking and sounding serious.

"Oh yes," Joanie answered, and she added, "at home we love our pets and we play with dogs and teach them tricks. Want to sees?" She called Findik. "Stay, stay," she commanded, pointing a teacher's finger at him. Findik stayed, with his bottom rising slightly from the ground in anticipation of the command. Joanie walked some feet from him. She picked up a stick and held it horizontally about six inches from the ground, then called, "Come on, boy!" Findik came as if flying, jumped over the stick. "Good boy!" she said, laughing and patting him.

Mr. Pudding stared blankly and straightened his turban that was constantly loose. "Hmmmm," he said. "Iss bedy American, tricks." He gathered his importance together, arms crossed, and he strutted away. Joanie was so pleased with Findik's performance that she hardly noticed the Captain.

She had seen me sitting on the front porch watching, and

with a straight back and a smiling face she walked over to me. "Isn't Findik smart?" she asked, then, "and isn't the Captain funny?"

"Funny," I said. "Bedy, bedy funny."

Mr. Pudding's Wife

Joan

JEANNE AND I WERE having a quiet cup of tea in the hot late afternoon when the gate bell rang. Jeanne went to the gate and I heard her say, "Do come in. Are you all right? Is there something the matter?"

It was Maruda, the wife of the army captain across the road. She came from Turkey. She was a pretty woman who was about to have her second baby.

Maruda glanced at us both, then at the door. "Please, you won't tell it my husband I have come here?" she said, in a quavering voice.

"Of course not," Jeanne said. "Please sit down." I went to the kitchen for another cup and when I returned, Maruda was rocking back and forth, holding her pregnant stomach. She did not wear the native abayah but a light cotton Western-style dress. Her hair was tousled and her eyes were bright with fear. She spoke English well and after a few sips of tea she grew somewhat calm. She began her story.

"Once, Madame, I was pretty woman in my home in Turkey and even I can be movie star." She told us she had once had a chance to go to the United States to be a stand-in for Bette Davis. "Now look at me; I am fat and ugly. I will choke to death in this Gehenna." She covered her face and rocked back and forth, back and forth. She told us more. "When I meet my husband he told it to me, if I marry him, I go to the beautiful city of Baghdad where there are some beautiful shops and clothes and many jewelries with silver and gold. I will have it servants and his mother will be my mother. He said we will be very happy in our home. Our home . . . " and she covered her face with her hands.

Such was the custom that when a young couple married, they made their home with the groom's parents, who took complete charge of the new family until her death, when the groom took over. To Maruda, who had lived simply all her life, Baghdad and its riches sounded exotic. She would be cared for and have all the silks and fashionable gowns she had ever dreamed of. "And I leave my job for movies and I marry him." Sobs overtook her and Jeanne tried to comfort her.

"Look," she said, "it's not too bad, really. You live in a nice home and you have a lovely little girl. Perhaps she'll soon have a baby brother."

Maruda moaned and kept her head down. "Brother, yes Madame, please pray for it a brother. My husband, he hates it baby girl. He says if I have girl he'll . . . " But sobs took away her voice and she could say no more.

Jeanne and I looked at each other. We were not being too helpful. "Will you go to the hospital near here so we can visit you?" I asked, trying to put across a positive thought.

"No hospital, Madame, only women in my room at home, screaming when I have it pain and drums making terrible noise." That crummy Captain, I thought, surely he has money for a hospital bed. "We don't have it any ether, Madame. Only screaming and screaming . . . I die seven times when I have it my baby girl. I know this time I die."

But Jeanne was persistent. "Perhaps it won't be so bad this time. The second child is always easier, you know."

Maruda stopped her sobbing for a moment and looked up. "Is true?" She looked at me for confirmation.

"It was for me, Maruda, and I bet it will be easier for you too."

She relaxed a little then, sat back, even drank a few sips of tea. Then she rose to go and she said, "Is really true, the second baby is not so bad pain?" I thought how pretty she was, even with her swollen eyes and her hair tousled and damp. So many tears. I wanted to pour some warmth and reassurance into her somehow, even a hug. But that was not the custom there and we nodded goodbye after Maruda thanked us and said again, "Please you will not tell my husband?"

Some weeks later we awoke to the beating of drums late in the night. Al and I crouched by our window—there was no sleeping. All the lights in the house across the road were on and the air around us felt electric. The sound was soft at first, then rose to a crescendo with the accompaniment of women's shrill voices. For seconds the drums beat fast and loud and the voices trilled on a high note. Then it all softened and I knew Maruda was in labor. I wondered if the sound was there to hide her screams. How wretched for the poor woman. The drum beats started again, and so it continued all night, like waves in a stormy sea, until just before dawn. All the time, though I knew praying for a boy was highly impractical, I found myself thinking, please Allah, for Maruda's sake, let it be a baby boy. There was suddenly a silence.

In minutes we heard ankle bracelets and bare feet beating on the dirt road. We saw men and women come dancing toward us, singing. One girl in the lead dipped her body and arms to the ground, up and back, her feet soft on the dust. She was a swan gliding on a quiet lake. There were others behind her, arm in arm, singing and swaying out a dance beat. We watched and listened until they were gone out of sight and sound.

It was just before dawn. As if summoned to herald the birth of a baby, the birds struck up their early morning concert and the sun made the sky a glowing pink. The household across the road was quiet. I knew somehow that Maruda had her little boy.

Around noon Mr. Pudding, Captain that he was, strutted across the road. Pride in every step. His servant followed him with the baby wrapped tightly with arms and legs straight down in swaddling clothes. He rang the gate bell and both our families came to the gate. "Madame, Doctor," he announced pompously, making a sweeping gesture to allow his servant to step forward. "My boy, izzent-it?" We congratulated him and Jeanne and I looked at each other and grinned happily, because we both knew that now Maruda could fall into a fearless sleep.

The Mosque at Khadhimain

Al

SAMMOUN IS THE flat pita-like bread sold in the streets of Baghdad. You can split it on the side and stuff meat and vegetables into it. The vendor carries it on a large circular tray on top of his head. He lowers the tray and rests it on a portable stand when he is about to make a sale. It makes an interesting picture. I obtained permission from a vendor to take his photograph on the street near the college.

I had just clicked the shutter when one of my students approached me angrily and asked, "Why are you taking pictures like that?"

"I think it's a picturesque sight," I said.

"That's not the real reason," he said. "You're taking it because you want to paint a bad picture of Iraq to show your Jewish friends when you go back to America. I've seen pictures in British magazines which portray us as backward Arabs." He had once heard me say that many of my boyhood friends in Brooklyn were Jewish.

At my request the student walked back to the college with me and we continued our discussion in my office. I said, "By the time I'm ready to leave Baghdad I think you'll believe me. I simply thought it was colorful and interesting." But his action had alerted me to a sensitivity about photography which I would soon learn was even more pronounced in other quarters.

The student continued, "If you want to shoot something

beautiful you should visit the Mosque at Khadhimain. It is a shrine which Muslim pilgrims come to visit from afar."

I had heard about Khadhimain from other students and from my neighbor, the army captain. In fact he had offered to take me to see it. Since he had failed to get me to go with him to Abdulla's night club he had proposed instead a visit to the Mosque at Khadhimain on condition that I didn't bring my harem with me. He couldn't get over the fact that I took my wife and three daughters with me wherever I went. For him, and for most men, Baghdad was a man's world.

I had read the following advice in an Army manual for U.S. military personnel in the Middle East: "When you pass by a mosque . . . keep walking." I asked Naseeb if it would be dangerous for me to visit a mosque.

"If they know you are not a Muslim it is certainly true in Iraq and especially so in Khadhimain. They are fanatical there. I have heard of Christians who have been stabbed to death because they had entered the area of the mosque in which only Muslims are allowed."

He went on to tell me that this was not the case in Cairo and in Istanbul, where visitors from all over the world are a common sight in the mosques. But Khadhimain was something else.

The Captain and I made a date for the following Friday at nine o'clock in the morning in front of my house. I said, "May I take my camera along? I'm very anxious to take photographs for my slide show."

"Well, that could be dangerous; but leave it to me. I'll arrange it. Just bring your camera along. The secret to success is to pass you off as an Arab. That shouldn't be too difficult."

We met at the appointed hour. The Captain was not wearing his uniform. He wore a western style suit and a green tie. He had also given me a green tie to wear that day. He explained, "The priests at Khadhimain are fond of this particular shade of green. It is based upon a tradition that goes back to the prophet. I figure it won't hurt for us to wear something green."

My camera, which I normally carried in a pocket, was

attached to a strap that went over my shoulder. The Captain had said that it was better to let it show than to carry it hidden. Pulling it out suddenly where it was not expected might raise suspicions and fear. "Just don't take any pictures until I give you a signal," he said.

We took a special bus that left us within walking distance of Khadhimain. This worked out quite well because the transition from the life style of Baghdad to that of Khadhimain was as drastic as that from Paris to Baghdad. During the next twenty minutes we walked backwards in time. The market place in Khadhimain could have been a Middle Eastern market in biblical times, except for the intrusion of an occasional bus carrying pilgrims.

The most prevalent mode of transport was the donkey. They would bump you out of their way as they passed you. I saw a barefooted Arab boy on a donkey riding away from us, his legs swinging in rhythm with the donkey's gait. I also saw a man riding a donkey while his barefooted wife wearing the black abayah walked a few paces behind him.

The Captain had been right about the color green. Priests walked around the marketplace wearing a red fez with a distinctive green band around it. We passed by an area where large pieces of green cloth, recently dyed, were spread out to dry.

From the marketplace you could get an occasional glimpse of the four minarets on the mosque a few blocks away. They were the tallest and most impressive towers I had seen. Each one had, about halfway up its slender shaft, a large circular balcony from which summons to prayer could be cried by the muezzins. It was called the golden mosque of Khadhimain. The spires were indeed golden and they glistened in the sunlight. This was the first time since we had arrived in Baghdad that I felt aesthetically moved by a work of art.

A true believer is supposed to make a pilgrimage to Mecca at least once in his lifetime. Khadhimain was a lesser shrine, but it attracted pilgrims from other countries as well as from other parts of Iraq. They came by the busload. These rickety conveyances were jammed with pilgrims dressed in much more colorful attire than we were used to in Baghdad. They came from such far away places as India and Iran.

The Captain pulled me into a side street that led to the mosque. He asked some strangers if I would be permitted to take photographs of the mosque. They asked, "Is he a Muslim?" The Captain hedged, "He is an Iraqi who was brought up in the United States. He was born here but he doesn't speak Arabic any more."

"Why don't you come to the roof of my house. He can get good pictures from there."

Another man interjected, "You can get the best angle from *my* house. The famous photograph that has appeared in many magazines was taken from there." The Captain said to me, "They want us to pay them a fee for the privilege. Come, let's move on."

We passed by some shops smelling of good food. "These are the famous kebab shops of Khadhimain," said the Captain. "We must visit one before we leave. Coming to Khadhimain without eating kebab is like going to Cairo without seeing the pyramids. The mosque is the big attraction but the kebab runs a close second."

The courtyard of the mosque was surrounded by a high wall with huge wooden doors at several gates guarded by men in long robes. "They are descendants of the prophet and their job is to guard the place," said the Captain. Their red fezzes had the green band characteristic of Khadhimain around them. The faces of these sons of the prophet had not felt the caress of a razor for days. They were not bearded; they were just unshaven. They reminded me of the bully in the Popeye comic. I was on pins and needles with fear.

The Captain and I walked slowly by one of the open gates, and I saw the interior courtyard for the first time. It was an awe-inspiring sight. It was as large as a football field. I could now see the entrance to the mosque. It had three rectangular sections with long thin columns, the outermost ones about three stories high and the central one even higher. The central domes and the bottom of the minarets were now visible in all their golden splendor. Pilgrims had removed their shoes, and several groups, each numbering in the hundreds, were kept within rectangular boundaries by their guides. There were two or three hundred pilgrims in each group, but the space was immense and did not look crowded. An air of electric expectation animated the multitude.

I was itching to ask the Captain if I could shoot but remembered not to speak English and held my peace. And now the guard near our entrance walked away for some unexpected reason. The Captain stepped into the courtyard but I didn't dare do so. I just kept watching him for a high sign.

Suddenly the Captain made the appropriate gesture and, without actually entering the courtyard, I raised my camera and took five pictures in rapid succession. I had never shot pictures under the influence of such mixed emotions of fear and awe. For an instant I experienced something of the spiritual exultation which the pilgrim, in the company of their fellows, must have felt.

I stayed near the door long enough to hear the muezzin begin his chant. The pilgrims kneeled, bowed, and prayed, following their leaders. I was moved by the emotional impact of the Muslim religious tradition.

The Captain stepped out of the doorway, took me by the arm, and without speaking guided me down the street that headed back toward the marketplace. When he felt safe to speak he said, "Did you get your pictures?"

I said, "I think I have five excellent shots."

"Let's go and have some kebab," said the Captain. "This is a good place. Doesn't it smell good? Let's go in." I knew he'd say that. The lamb *did* smell delicious, but I was afraid I'd end up with a case of "Baghdad tummy."

The first thing that struck me about the place was the primitive workmanship of floors, tables, and chairs. The floors were not level, the tables leaned, no two chairs were of the same design, and they were all rickety.

I asked the Captain to put in my order without parsley but he said it would be more diplomatic to order the works and simply not eat the parsley. The Captain took everything—all sorts of colorful relishes, beets, sauces, parsley, and lamb. He stuffed it into the sliced sammoun bread and bit hungrily into the mountain of food he held with both hands. I was very hungry, but I ate only the sammoun and the kebab. I must admit it was delicious and that if I had been served the same dish in a clean hotel I would probably have eaten it heartily and enjoyed it thoroughly. But here I felt everything was dirty. The plaster walls were not perfectly vertical so they had accumulated the dust of ages on their inclined surfaces. Wherever I looked I saw piles of dirt. To me Iraq was a dirty place and Khadhimain was no exception.

Fortified with food we walked back to the marketplace. The Captain, knowing I wanted to take home some souvenirs, stopped one of the vendors carrying a tray of trinkets. "Let's see what you have there," he said in Arabic. The tray was full of rings and bracelets. Nothing looked particularly attractive to me. Some were made of plastic and I thought to myself, "These were probably made in Passaic, New Jersey." They were certainly not typical of Iraq, but the Captain handled them, picked a few and said, "Here, I'm going to buy a ring for each of your daughters."

The vendor did not object when the Captain handled the goods but when I picked up one of the trinkets the peddler was suddenly very angry, yanked the trinket away from me, and put if off to one side. The peddler had been suspicious of me from the start. I had probably inadvertently spoken a few words of English.

We walked away so the peddler could not hear me. I asked the Captain, "Why was he so angry?" The Captain said, "He suspected you are not a Muslim. By touching the trinket you made it unclean. He will not be able to sell it until it is purified by going through a ritual that will last several weeks."

I had encountered a new perception of cleanliness.

Once A City Called Babylon

Joan

IT WAS SPRING. We were all well. No one had Baghdad
Tummy. Joanie's shades of yellow jaundice had finally faded
like a healed scar. The sun was drying up the mud so that we
could walk on the roads again.

Some of the students warned Al one day. "Dr. Baez, you will
please stay away from the University tomorrow, Sair. It will be
dangerous for you because it is our annual day of protest."

We had heard of the day that the Arabs took vengeance on
the Jews for a persecution that had happened many years
before. On this day there would be rioting in the streets, fires
set, bricks and stones thrown. all this in and around the
University building because it was the students who organized
it. They had become devoted to Al and they wanted no harm to
come to him.

Naseeb, always coming up with ideas for entertainment on a
day off, said to Al, "Dr. Baez, Sair,"—he wore his most
endearing smile— "this is a good opportunity for you to take
your family to Babylon. Iz-*zent* it? I will hire a car and we will
go together. This is ancient history the children should not miss.
You know it is more than two thousand years old. The great
citadel there was the center of culture, law, and entertainment.

This was a very beautiful city. I think your children would like it very much." How could Al refuse?

We were up while the air was still cool, the sky a glowing pink umbrella, and the town quiet. Off we bounced in a battered British taxi, over a white hot plate of sand that within the hour reached a temperature of 102 degrees. For miles around us a thick pall of dust hung just above the surface of the sand like a golden smog, far, far into the flat distance. Now and then, way out there, a lonely tree shimmered in the fiery furnace. Here and there we waved to a family of Bedouins who sat in front of their tents like statues. Being wise about the heat, they never moved unless it was necessary. Only their heads turned to watch our passing car.

Farther on we followed a strip of road, bordered on both sides by green grass, evidence of a last trickle of the Tigris River that had flowed by the forgotten city of Babylon.

We approached the hill on which the once-beautiful city had thrived. The driver told Naseeb, when we bumped over a small rise, that now we were on the grounds where the great citadel had stood.

A gatekeeper, who wore a long brown robe and whose face had the appearance of wadded up brown paper with holes in the right places, stopped us and exchanged words with our driver. We parked the car under a dwarf eucalyptus tree. The driver made ready for a nice long sleep and the rest of us followed the old man as he beckoned us on. He spoke directly to Naseeb, waving a brown bony arm, pointing to where we may and we may not go. Naseeb translated, "Our man says we must stay together. We must not go near the caves." He pointed to what must have been ruins, rocks, and boulders in disarray down an incline a short distance from us. Naseeb went on, "There are wild dogs and jackals down there and they become vicious when they're frightened. They are very afraid of people." It was an eerie quiet we all felt as we moved around. Mimi moved close to Joanie.

Al picked up a small chip of aquamarine pottery. "Pretty," he said to the gatekeeper, who turned to Naseeb and said something angrily. Naseeb nodded wisely, then smiled at Al and muttered, "Dr. Baez, Sair, l think it is better you drop this or our man is going to beat you." Al made a pretense at being serious and gently laid the precious chip on the ground. Naseeb explained then that once the whole area had been covered with these beautiful pieces of ceramic. "It is difficult to imagine, Dr. Baez, that in the year 2,000 B.C. these tiny chips were pots for water and vases for flowers that were used everywhere. This city was famous for its beautiful colors and designs." He went on to tell us that the old man had become angry because the tourists had almost divested the grounds of them. "You see, everything here is precious to this man. He owns Babylon, really." He smiled broadly.

Al bowed slightly as a gesture of apology to the old man who turned and strode away with his crooked walking stick.

Al and Naseeb remained sitting on a rock in full view of us while we wandered toward the caves, the tumbled ruins. We promised to be quiet. We just wanted to peek. There was a frightening attraction about them.

"It's spooky," Mimi said. She was right. I had the feeling that some grinning monster would rise from the depths of those echoing rocks, snarl ferociously, and whisk us away on sound-less feet, or a herd of jackals would come snarling and growling, frothing at the mouth and grab our feet. But there was not a sound down there.

"I guess the animals are sleeping," Joanie said, with a bit of a shake in her voice.

"Shall we just leave them alone?" Mimi suggested. With no hesitation, we tiptoed over the hot sand to see where the Hanging Gardens of Hammurabi had once adorned the balconies and pathways around the great citadel. All the time something in a far-off section of my brain was saying, this too was a part of the Garden of Eden. God's chosen slice of the world. It must have been a splendid sight. Not now, though. The gardens of the Fertile Crescent had given way to dry grasses in hot sand.

After crossing a small rise in the ground, we were entirely

alone. The only sounds were the wind whining through the rocks and ruins, the jackals now and then yipping as if in their sleep, and the whirring wings of hawks and vultures that flew close and perched on the tips of rocks. They watched with greedy eyes as if waiting for one of us to drop. I saw Mimi take hold of Joanie's hand.

The intense heat, the white sky and the hollow gardens gave me a deadweight feeling of oppression. No one spoke as we walked back to the trees. Perhaps our spirits were dampened by the emptiness that centuries of destruction had left.

Popsy called, "Lunch time!"

Good, that brought us back to right now and our gurgling stomachs. We uncovered our baskets, beckoned the old gatekeeper to join us, and we sat near his hut eating oranges, dates, and sammoun with butter and jam, and we drained a large thermosful of lemon squash.

As we drove away, the gatekeeper, no longer angry, or perhaps happy that we were leaving, put the palms of his hands together and bowed to us. He belonged to the craggy rocks, the ancient walls, and the eucalyptus trees. The ruins of the old city all belonged to him. It was empty and peaceful now. I would never again hear a jackal or a wild dog's hollow bark, or hear the crows' and vultures' eerie cries without thinking of them watching the old man hungrily.

"I bet he gets lonesome in that spooky place," Mimi said. "I would. Aren't you glad we don't live there, Mum?"

The Royal Hunt Club

Al

MR. BADEE, WHO TAUGHT chemistry at the college, was a member of the military equestrian reserve. He popped into my office one day and asked, "Do any of your girls ride horses?" He had heard that our neighbor in Al Waziria had a horse and allowed my children to feed and stroke him.

"All three of them do," I replied. "They're crazy about horses. A friend of ours at Stanford University taught them how to ride."

"Well I'm going to see that you are all invited to attend a fox hunt and the next exhibition of horsemanship sponsored by the Royal Hunt Club. Do you think your girls would like that?"

"They will go out of their minds with joy," I said.

The girls were all excited when I broke the news to them at the dinner table. The Regent, who ruled Iraq while young King Faisal II was being educated in England, was to be the guest of honor at both occasions. That did not excite the girls as much as the fantasy of seeing beautiful examples of what the term "Arabian horse" conjured up in their minds.

We had seen very few good horses in Baghdad. The poor, beat-up nags that pulled the arabanas were a sorry sight. They were maimed, decrepit, and skinny and had sores all over them. When you rode in an arabana you felt sorry for the horse and wondered if he'd ever make it. We looked forward to seeing better looking horses at the Royal Hunt Club.

My daughters were all still children, but Pauline was on the verge of young womanhood. She was very pretty and, at thirteen, noticeably taller than the other two. She had the lightest skin of all three and hair that had been almost blonde as a child. She was also the most reserved. Mr. Badee had seen a photograph of the three girls and had been quite taken by Pauline. He wanted her to ride on the hunt with him. In order to deal with the invitation in a diplomatic manner he invited all of us to attend, but only Pauline was to actually participate in the hunt. She would, in fact be the only female rider. Pauline's beauty and the unusual circumstances that had brought her to Baghdad gave Mr. Badee the green light to break all the rules and invite her to ride.

"She doesn't have a proper riding outfit," I said to Badee.

"It doesn't matter," he said. "She can wear anything that's comfortable." So, for the occasion, Pauline designed and sewed a colorful shirt and pants made of a plaid material she had found in the zuc.

The appointed day for the hunt was a Friday, a holy day for religious Muslims. But for our party it began with drinks at ten in the morning at the estate of Mrs. Page, a charming and elegant looking Englishwoman who was hosting the event. The British lived well in Baghdad. There was whiskey and wine for the adults and Coca-Cola and squash for the children. The men were part of an elite military clique. They were all well-fed, healthy, and athletic army officers or members of the reserves. I noticed that the Muslim prohibition of alcoholic drinks didn't seem to deter any of the people at this gathering. (In Baghdad only the poor seemed to observe religious customs in public. I saw only beggars in tatters and farashes kneeling in prayer in the street when the muezzin chanted from the minaret.)

Heels clicked as the Regent, wearing a red jacket and jodhpurs, got out of his Rolls Royce to meet Mrs. Page. Everyone stood up. He wore dark glasses and a white scarf which stuck out of his neckline like Kleenex popping from its box. He was not an impressive looking man but he represented the Royal Family in the absence of the King. He made a perfunctory tour of Mrs. Page's mansion which housed equestrian trophies in glass-covered show-cases. Many of these were "brushes"— fox-tails with the name of the winner engraved on their silver handles.

All the riders, except Pauline, were dressed in riding gear with proper jodhpurs, boots, dashing red coats—the works. Pauline stood out, not only because she was the sole woman, but because her normally white skin was smoothly tanned and she had the blossom of youth. Her informal attire only added to her charm.

Before long the Regent headed back to his Rolls Royce. This was the signal for people to drop what they were doing and get into their cars. We rode with Mr. Badee and some officers in a bus and headed south in the direction of what was euphemistically called "New Baghdad." It looked like a desert to us.

When we arrived, the Army flunkies who had groomed the horses were now lined up holding them, waiting for their masters to mount up. Others held the hounds on leash. Hounds, horns, and red coats made it look like England, but it also had a touch of Hollywood.

Badee was busy making bets—the exact nature of which I did not understand—with the other riders. Later I learned he was betting that Pauline would survive the perils of the hunt and maneuver her horse without falling off.

Joan said to Mr. Badee, "Please take care of Pauline. She's very young, you know. She's quite skilled at riding but she's never participated in a hunt before."

"Don't worry, Mrs. Baez, I'll ride beside her all the way. If I see she's getting tired she and I can ride around slowly while the hunt proceeds."

Pauline looked beautiful mounted on her horse—a dark brown Arabian stallion—and she rode it like an expert. She had been told that the first rider to spy the fox would be awarded his tail—the brush—so she was on the lookout for him from the word go. Somewhere ahead the poor little fox had been released.

The horn was sounded. The hunt had begun!

Now Joan, Joanie, Mimi and I had several hours to kill. It was going to be a scorching hot day. We were told that a horse race would take place at a nearby track so we walked over to it. It was the only source of entertainment left for us. It was a poor man's racetrack, unlike the elegant one at the northern end of town. Nevertheless, a holiday mood prevailed. The men spent their time sizing up the horses, arguing, eating, spitting, choosing a winner and betting. The trainers led their horses around to show them off to the spectators.

Joanie made friends with a cute little Arab boy. He couldn't speak a word of English but somehow we managed to understand what he was trying to tell us. He was a stable boy whose master owned a horse that would run in the race. He wanted us to bet on him. He couldn't understand why we had come if we were not going to bet at all. His master, who owned the horse, was dressed up like a beat-up old sheik. His long robe was dirty. I took a picture of him with the boy and Joanie and Mimi but I couldn't get him to smile. He was so ugly that I was afraid he would break the lens.

We waited a full two hours under a blazing sun for the race to start. We discovered, to our surprise, that the Regent had not gone off on the hunt. He was leaning against a rail at the track, ready to watch the race. He didn't see us.

Now, when we least expected it, we saw in the distance within the race track what looked for all the world like a tornado whose vortex was filled with dust from the ground. It approached us silently and very rapidly, but when this dust storm passed right in front of us we could hear the clatter of racing hooves going along with it. We still did not see a thing except dust, but the sounds told us that the race horses were enveloped by this cloud. It rushed past and then away from us as rapidly as it had approached, until we could still see the tornado but could no longer hear the roll of the horses' hooves.

The race, for which we had waited more than an hour, was

over in a matter of minutes. I have no idea how they determined who had won inside this impenetrable envelope of dust, but for the next hour or so the spectators were busy collecting winnings from their bets and starting to make new ones in preparation for a race that would follow, probably an hour later.

We went back to where the hunt had started. In the distance we saw the riders returning. Pauline was among the first. She looked all flushed, sunburnt, and happy. Mr. Badee was jolly. Pauline, his protégé, had not let him down. She had ridden all the way, jumped when necessary and had not fallen off the horse. She would be awarded the brush that day, and Mr. Badee had won at least 20 dinars in bets that day.

Now Badee called the Master of the Hunt and Pauline to join him in having their pictures taken. The Master of the Hunt was a most impressive looking Arab. He was very tall and dark. His black boots made him look even taller. He wore a red jacket, but his headgear was made of an orange cloth held on his head with a black cord. He looked much more regal than the Regent and more aristocratic than most of the lantern-jawed British people I met in Baghdad. He made me think of an ancient Arab monarch—dignified and straight-backed. He bowed politely when he was introduced and when he smiled he displayed a picket fence of gold teeth that shone in the sun.

Badee had arranged to have him handing the brush to Pauline while we all took photographs. It was, especially for Pauline, a fitting climax to a day that had begun in uncertainty.

We had not yet had lunch and it was already about two o'clock in the afternoon. We were famished. We all drove back to Mrs. Page's house where a huge banquet had been laid out on long tables out of doors. Nothing could begin however, because the Regent had not returned. There were about five tables, each about twenty feet long, filled with huge dishes full of food. There was an entire sheep on one table and a huge fish on another. There were different kinds of rice and many vegetables.

All the riders washed their hands meticulously and then sat

and chatted with one another and with us until the Regent arrived, at which time everyone stood again. The Regent, after washing, went straight to one of the tables. That was the sign for everyone else to do the same. Mr. Badee took Pauline in tow, and each of us had a temporary host to initiate us into the food ceremony.

The Regent took a fistful of rice and put it on his plate. Only then could all the rest begin to do the same, and we lost no time in doing so. We were all ravenous. The officer nearest each member of my family took a fistful of rice and put it on our plates. I noticed that Mr. Badee was doing the same for Pauline. Then they took a chunk of lamb, still steaming hot, out of the huge pile and put it on our plates. Once we got the idea we began putting food on our own plates the same way.

There were no knives or forks. You took the rice and the meat off your plate with your hands and put it into your mouth. We were clumsy at it initially and peeked at one another to see how we were managing with this technique.

The members of my family took our plates to our seats nearby, but we noticed that everyone else just stood near the food tables and ate standing up. About fifty people stayed near the tables continuing to put food on their plates with their hands and then into their mouths. Nobody talked. They just stuffed and guzzled.

There was a great variety of cakes and fruit. Tangerines—called mandarins here—were plentiful. I must have eaten about ten of them. The custom was to peel the tangerine while you stood near the table and throw the peels on the ground. We couldn't get ourselves to do it at first until we saw Joanie doing it. She was enjoying it the way a child enjoys doing something naughty for which he knows he will not get punished. The guests went through the piles of fruit like vultures on meat. When Joan came in search of a tangerine they were all gone. Pits, skins and leftovers from all the fruit and meat were on the lawn. It looked like a battlefield the day after the war.

Mr. Badee came over and said, "His Royal Highness is asking about your daughter Pauline," making it sound like a line from a fairy tale. The Regent came over and congratulated Pauline on having been awarded the brush. She accepted the compliment graciously but with a minimum of words.

And now the official photographers got busy, following the Regent around and taking pictures of him as he talked to different people including our family. But when the moment came to take the official photograph of this memorable day at the Royal Hunt Club, which included the Regent, the Master of the Hunt, Mr. Badee, and the Officers of the Club, the only member of our family invited to participate, for obvious reasons, was Pauline.

Several weeks later Mr. Badee invited all of us to a public exhibition of horsemanship. This time students from the college, dressed in western-style suits, sat in the stands and poor children from the town, dressed in what looked to us like nightgowns, sat on top of a stone wall. In the distance there was a special stand for the Queen, but it was empty. The few women in attendance were out there in the distance, covered from head to toe with the black abayahs.

The most colorful group was the Royal Iraqi Band, which played, to our surprise, some Sousa marches, including "The Stars and Stripes Forever" and "Semper Fidelis." The equestrian exhibits included riders spearing an object on the ground. One of the horses was severely injured in a jump and had to be shot on the spot. This was a terrible shock to us.

The Regent sat in a special Royal Stall behind us but near enough to recognize our family. We all observed that when Pauline looked back in his direction he nodded discreetly.

That was the last time we saw the Regent. Political uprisings had begun to sweep through Iraq. Public outrage against those in power who had close ties with the British began to emerge. One day my children, riding home in the Presentation School bus, saw four men hanging in the public square near the North Gate. This was the harbinger of activities that would eventually culminate in the assassination of the King. After we left Baghdad we read that the Regent's body had been dragged through the streets.

Good Christian Spinach

Joan

EARLY IN JUNE, the tiny green spears of spinach peeked through the surface of the areas of seeded fields that surrounded our Baghdad home. As the days fell behind us, the fields turned from mud-brown to a rich green. Our homes, huts, and long dusty roads were entrances and exits to acres of spinach.

Wives of the impoverished farmers who cultivated the fields for landlords carried baskets of spinach on their heads. Their children toddled after them, dragging baskets of the momentarily life-giving substance in their arms. Spinach to sell. The law even allowed these farmers to keep a small amount of their produce.

One hot, dry morning, as I picked the little black pebbles out of our rice, I heard a low, dull-voiced "Memsah." I spun around, and there in the doorway was a tall woman. She had come in so softly on her broad bare feet that I hadn't noticed her. She looked regal in spite of unwashed hands and face, protruding pregnant stomach, and her ragged black abayah. "Memsah, *schpint*." (Memsah, spinach.)

Her face was partially covered with her unclean garment, and at her side were two expressionless small children, eyes wide and staring, noses running and mouths gaping. They held tightly to their mother's skirts and in the tall woman's arms was a small baby girl. She too stared listlessly. Not at me—not at anything. Her chin and the stained cloth that covered her tiny chest and stomach were wet with drool; her hair was henna-colored and stuck to her head in clotted lumps of mud. It was a custom to dye the hair henna from the flowering bush whose leaves, when boiled, produced a reddish colored water. After coloring the hair they managed to roll it in little circles and stick it to their heads with mud. There was a tiny gold ring pierced into one side of the wee baby's nostril. I thought to myself, how would they ever wipe that nub of a nose without her screaming with pain?

"Memsah, schpint?" The woman repeated, and she held out her basket full and heavy with fresh green leaves.

She wanted to sell it, mud and all, I thought, and why not?

"Memsah, me Chris," she dared half a smile.

I spoke slowly. "You are a Christian?" I made the sign of the cross and pointed to her.

"Na'am," (yes), she nodded, and a flicker of hope lightened her eyes.

"This is schpint, and you want flus?"

She shook her head, "la-la," (no, no), and her face grew brighter as she held out her basket to me. I understood then. She was giving it to me, taking a chance that perhaps, just perhaps, I would give her something to eat in return.

"No flus?" I smiled at her, took the basket, and dumped the muddy spinach into the sink. "All right, you wait right there like a good Christian, and I'll see if there's anything . . . " I went on muttering to myself, alternately smiling at her and poking around in our family stash of canned goods. She'd surely like sweet things like peaches, pears, figs, and of course, dates. I even dared a small jar of peanut butter. I held it up to her and made "mmmmm good" noises of approval and rubbed my stomach. "Great protein," I mumbled, and shoved it into the basket along with some pistachio nuts and powdered milk. As I looked up again her face had momentarily lost its anxiety.

"You could be a madonna," I said out loud when an awful

thought and a pang of conscience interrupted my fun. If Jeanne were to walk into this scene she would go weak-kneed and drop from shock. I picked up the basket, pushed it into the woman's hands, turned her children toward the door and whispered, "Fi aman el lah" (goodbye). I kept a wary eye on all entrances as I quickly accompanied her to the gate. She took time to turn, put the basket down for a moment, face her palms together and bow her head.

"Ashkurich," she murmured her thanks; then she and her tiny troop were gone and I relaxed. But only for a moment; because as I returned to the kitchen and saw the green mountain in the sink, I thought—what in God's name could we do with all that?

That was only the beginning of a spinach saga that lasted for weeks. When she caught the poor woman slithering out of the gate one day, Jeanne was icily polite. I was apologetic.

"She's so stupid," Jeanne complained in her British accent, her face a map of frowns. "How can she expect us to eat all that awful stuff?" She held her round pregnant stomach as if the idea nauseated her. She never complained about it, but I knew how she felt.

"I guess she's hungry," I attempted to explain.

"Then why doesn't *she* eat it?"

"Maybe she wants to share, Jeanne," and we both laughed.

The problem only grew each day as my lady left the green mounds at the gate, whether she received recompense or not. We might have stashed it in Jeanne's Kelvinator refrigerator, as Jeanne had been kind enough to let us use half of it, but fill it with spinach? Hardly a wise move. If we put the greens in the garbage, the "Chris-woman's" children who sat beside the enormous, foul-smelling pail to pick up crumbs and bits of old food would find it. We couldn't do that. If we buried it, the workmen who were always about and always curious might discover it and tattle. So I thought the problem finally well solved when I stuffed bunches of it into the cement box that housed the water-heating device. Good, now it would dry and vanish, I hoped. But the ever-hungry cats were attracted to the juice in those spinach leaves and soon they dragged it all over the back yard. I even dreamed my mouth was so filled with spinach that I could neither swallow nor spit it out. Spinach consumed both day and night.

One day Jeanne took the bull by the horns and called Mahal and told him in well-clipped tones—if not perfect Arabic—to "get that beastly woman out of here." Mahal clucked and cackled maliciously, his one red eye dancing like a flame.

The morning he spied her I shrank into the shadow of the doorway as he shooed her off, stick in hand, voice croaking like the night frogs. He cussed her until she and her babes were far out of sight. Poor woman, we could do no more for her.

That afternoon we planned our next move: Jeanne, all our children, and I filled our baskets with the now-withered, limp leaves, covered them with towels, and, keeping our eyes watchful on all sides for the curious, pussyfooted our way to the only real car at our end of town, Jeanne's car. We crammed the dratted stuff into it and drove away.

We traveled across town, beyond the houses to the thirsty fields where a few gaunt cows ruminated on dry weeds. There we dumped the last of our Christian schpint in a big heap and hurried away just as the cows with the white glazed-doughnut eyes meandered toward us. Home we went to a leafless kitchen. It was only once in a while afterwards, when I walked down the dusty road, that I would hear a familiar voice, muffled by a black abayah, say "Saba, Memsah, saba" (hello, Memsah, hello).

The Departure

Al

THE UNIVERSITY TERM was coming to an end. The days had become unbearably hot. The end of our stay in Baghdad was imminent. I had been working frantically on writing and administering final examinations and supervising the last details of the painting and furnishings of the new physics labs. I began to think it would be nice to have an open house ceremony before leaving.

Dean Duri had pleaded with me to stay another year, but I felt my daughters had to get back into the educational stream at Redlands. They had clearly suffered a setback in their academic education, although the impact of their one year in Baghdad would last for the rest of their lives. Joanie in particular had experienced severe health problems. Mimi had been dealt a blow by the insensitive and cruel way Sister Rose had handled her reading disability. Pauline had suffered the least. Life had not been pleasant for her either, but she had actually gained weight and not been ill treated at school.

Joan had borne the vicissitudes of an uncomfortable year in silence and with outward good grace, but she too had had enough and was anxious to get home. She missed her house and garden in Redlands. She had not really wanted to come to Baghdad but had done so for my sake. She would some day follow me again to other distant places when she would rather have stayed at home, and that would build up a resentment which would one day generate a disaster. I was completely unaware of this at the time. I knew only that the tension built up in one year in Baghdad, coupled with the anxiety of preparations for departure, had exhausted her.

We had about two weeks to go and were frantically trying to solve all the details associated with pulling up stakes. We had found heavy steel footlockers in the zuc to carry bulky items like the oriental rugs we had bought for each member of the family. We had come to terms with Ali concerning large items which he would keep. But we still had quite a bit of furniture, such as beds and chairs, which Ali could not use and did not wish to buy.

I explained my plight to Alan Peters and he said, "As a last resort you might consider Dalwisha. He's an auctioneer. He buys and sells furniture. I think he's fairly honest."

So I called up Dalwisha and explained my plight. Dalwisha said, "I've heard about you, Doctor Baez. You're with Unesco, aren't you? I'll send my representative over this afternoon to appraise your furniture."

To my surprise the representative turned out to be Jack, the Iraqi with an American accent whose trajectory had intersected with ours on more than one occasion. Jack had appeared out of nowhere in the very first days when we were looking for a house. He had helped other American families working for the State Department to find homes in Baghdad. At that time we had not dealt with Jack for two reasons. One was that my Unesco salary was not as high as those of the State Department types. The other was that Ali, the Arab with a British accent, could not stand this upstart Jack-of-all-trades—an Iraqi with a coarse American accent—who threatened to do for a price what Ali felt he could do alone. Jack had dropped out of our lives for a while after we moved into the house in Al Waziria.

But Jack had popped up again when I was looking for a painter. Father Connell had recommended ICI paints for the lab walls in preference to the kalsomine paints which had started to peel off my office walls. The ICI people had told me they would send their representative over to see me and, lo and behold, it turned out to be the notorious Jack-of-all-trades.

Now here was Jack again, popping up like a Jack-in-the-box, this time as the representative of Dalwisha, the auctioneer. I too had resented Jack's brash and cocky ways, but remembered that he *had* been helpful in the past.

"Well, Doctor Baez," said Jack. "How nice to see you again. How can I help you this time?"

"Hello, Jack," I said. "I've got a house full of furniture I must sell before I leave. Can you help me?"

"Why, of course," said Jack as he walked through the rooms and sized up what we had. He jotted down a few notes and said he would have Dalwisha ring me that afternoon.

Dalwisha made me an offer. It was low, I felt, but there was no use in haggling. He would take everything off my hands and I could keep my furniture until the last minute. We made a deal. It was a tremendous load off my mind. Jack's uncouth manners had rubbed me the wrong way at times but I had to concede that, once again, he had helped me.

ONE WAY TO ENSURE that a projected task gets done is to establish a deadline for its completion. It works best if it is associated with a ceremonial event to which you have invited some dignitaries. That way there is no way to back out.

I went to the Dean and said: "Dean Duri, I am scheduled to leave Baghdad in about two weeks. The physics laboratory is almost finished. Don't you think it would be a good idea to have an opening ceremony to which we could invite the Minister of Education so he can see what we have done with the funds he allocated for this project?"

Duri said, "Right you are, Professor Baez, right you are. It's a jolly good idea. It would give me a chance to see it, too!" Duri had, in fact, been so busy at the end of the term that he hadn't had the time to walk over to the lab building three blocks away.

He suddenly sensed it would be a minor coup for him to host the Minister and show him what was now probably the best equipped college physics teaching lab in Iraq. He added, "I think we should also invite Father Connell of the Baghdad College, who gave us so much help in the early days, as well as other important people in educational circles in Baghdad." Duri was warming up to the public relations potential of the open house.

I agreed with him but I also wanted my physics students to attend so they could see what facilities would be available to them after I left. They had had to do their lab work in the winter in cold and bare rooms without easy access to such necessities as water and electricity. I wanted them to share in the pleasure of this event.

Dean Duri agreed, and before long we had a list of about sixty people. He said, "The weather should be pleasant. We could hold the ceremony at the end of the day, when it starts to cool off. We should have light refreshments and invite the guests to stay after the ceremony for a little party."

I was delighted to see the Dean beginning to take this over as his project. His policies had not always met with favor among the authorities. Jealousy over his successes also played a part. This event might help to smooth things over and win him the support he needed.

The Minister of Education accepted Dean Duri's invitation. That put the pressure on all of us to see that everything in the lab was shipshape. For the next two weeks we all worked at a feverish pace. Shauki and Amelda worked overtime. Sue Gray Al Salam cranked up the x-ray diffraction unit. The students who had volunteered to act as guides practiced demonstrating the new equipment.

On the appointed day farashes brought couches and chairs from the college and arranged them on the lawn outside the lab building. In the garden there were a few small flowering pepper trees, a little grass and nothing more. They strung up the electric lights. They set up tables for refreshments. Everyone helped. It was like a holiday.

When it began to get dark the early birds—mostly students— began to arrive and the student guides practiced their demonstrations on them. We knew the dignitaries would come last. Since the walls, tables, and cabinets had only recently been painted, everything looked and smelled fresh.

We had expected sixty visitors; more than a hundred came. The farashes had to scurry to get more Coca-Cola and ice cream. The visitors sat and chatted in little enclaves after coming out of the lab building. Dean Duri showed up last and I had the honor of escorting him myself through the various rooms of the lab. He was genuinely surprised at the transformation that had taken place. He filled his pipe repeatedly and smiled a great deal between puffs.

As we walked out of the building we noticed that everyone was standing. That could only mean that the Minister had arrived. His eyes bulged, as usual, but he also smiled as he nodded left and right. Dean Duri went over to meet him and bring him over to the steps of the building.

The Minister greeted me most cordially. Duri said to me, "Please escort the Minister personally through the laboratory. You are both responsible for its existence."

The Minister was accustomed to ceremonial occasions like this, but I was certain he had never visited a physics laboratory before. I introduced him to the students who performed demonstrations for him. I took him to the room which I facetiously called the analytical balance museum because it was full of analytical balances. Professor Nooh had ordered many more than would ever be needed in a physics laboratory. But, since everything looked shiny and new, it created a good impression. Like a good politician, the Minister spent as much time looking at people and smiling as he did in looking at the facilities.

By now it was dark and the string of electric lights had once again performed its magic. We were in a garden of delights where imperfections noticeable during the day were now invisible. The night was balmy. I took the Minister over to where Father Connell was sitting. The Right Reverend Archdeacon Roberts and the directors of the British Institute and the USIS were there. As Father Connell had said to me earlier,

"You will always see the same set of people at these occasions. Baghdad is really a small place."

The Minister who was known for his short speeches, spoke in Arabic. I was told that he praised the Dean and then me for the role we had played in bringing about the construction of the lab. He said just the right things. The crowd applauded and he sat down.

In the semi-darkness I could see the farashes huddled around the refreshments and helping themselves to tea, Coca-Cola, and ice cream. The ice cream was ultra sweet and syrupy and a ghastly green and red in color; but my children had been dying to have ice cream, so we threw all caution to the winds and ate it with abandon.

The students provided the entertainment. Kurdish students from the north of Iraq wore their colorful costumes. Some wore elaborate headgear much bigger than their heads. They played a string instrument which looked like a mandolin with a big belly. Others played flutes. Only the men danced. They formed a circle and held hands. They were much more colorful than the Baghdadis.

Some women students recited long poems. We asked what they were about and were told "love." But it was clear that some of them were eulogies to Baghdad. The long drawn out "Baghda-a-a-a-d" sounded like an extended sigh. One girl, who had a reputation for writing fiery poems, brought the house down with laughter and, in the end, terrific applause.

We learned later that this was the same girl who had been reprimanded earlier in the term for writing poems which were critical of the link between religion and the state. The priests in the mosques up and down Rashid Street had preached sermons about what a godless place the College of Arts and Sciences had become. They pointed a critical finger at Dean Duri for permitting this. The girl was prudent enough, however, in the presence of the Minister, to stick to humorous rather than political themes. The Minister took his leave when all eyes were concentrated on the entertainers, but when the students noticed that he had left they became even more relaxed and formed little groups around their favorite teachers.

When the musicians ran out of steam they started playing worn and scratched up old 78s with Arabic music on them through a public address system of low fidelity, high distortion, and monstrous volume. It rivaled the din we normally heard on Rashid Street but, as usual, nobody except my family seemed to notice or to mind.

In the midst of this noise I stopped to reflect that all this would soon be over. In two days we would be boarding a plane for Switzerland. I went off to one side where I could let my gaze wander slowly at the Dean, my students, the farashes, and visitors like Father Connell. I had developed a special relationship with people like Naseeb Dajani, Hassan Ahmed Hassan, Shauki, and Amelda, and I felt a glow of affection for them. I realized that I had made friends in Baghdad and would miss them.

"We're Going Home!"

Joan

SPRING WAS BURNING its way into summer and the thought of home beckoned just beyond the day's chores. Al was to return to his professorship at the University of Redlands, California. He looked thin and weary, even walked tired, and he had never done that. I, too, was drooping, but the wing feathers of my spirit fluttered with excitement.

Ilyas helped us at every turn. He told me that his sisters were professional seamstresses. "They are sewing beautiful dresses all the time for the rich people in town. Would you like them to make some dresses for you?" Good idea, I thought. The girls and I marched off to the zuc and bought enough material for all four of us to have dresses. The material was imported from England—cotton of excellent quality.

Then one blazing afternoon when the thermometer read 112 degrees Fahrenheit, away we bounced on a bus to the other end of town and found our way to an open-sewer street and the home of Ilyas and his family. We were greeted with gestures, lots of smiles, and nervous laughter. Ilyas was not at home. His family ushered us into their house. It was dark in the tiny living room and very close. The women gestured us to sit on the wicker chairs around the room. The five of them served us first a large tray of fresh fruit. We were careful to choose only the types that we could peel—oranges, bananas, and tangerines. Next they served us homemade cake (we were almost used to the taste of semne, their buffalo butter), and of course, lemon squash. All this eating was a necessary ritual. We had become quite used to it. Sometimes I even looked forward to it. When they served the coffee to Pauline and me and tea to Joanie and Mimi, that meant the social part of our visit was over. Much like buying carpets from Mr. Al Persia: after the coffee, we got down to business.

While we ate and gestured by way of communication, I looked around the room. There were the treadle sewing machine, the primitive shelving on the walls for their fabrics, a long wooden table, and a wall mirror. Those bits of furniture, plus our chairs, comprised the interior decorating of the living room in their home. I knew the bathroom facilities must be primitive because of the pungent odor of Lysol. That, combined with the semne cooking oil, kept me hoping there would be no outburst of giggles from my girls. It would be so typical for Mimi to hold her nose and say noisily, "eee-yuuu, what's that turble smell?" and send the other girls into stomach-holding hysterics. But she didn't; the saints had heard my plea.

Now to the measurements. The five sisters were quick and deft with pins, tape measure, and scissors. Their talk was aimed mostly at Mimi, whom they favored. "This little one iss bery beautiful," they would comment every now and then. I wish I could remember some of the Arabic words and sentences Mimi spoke with them, in a perfect accent.

We left when the measuring was finished. We bowed, waved, and called "ashkurich-ashkurich," promising to send American fashion magazines when we got home.

A few days later there was Ilyas, all smiles and a huge box full of new dresses. It amazed me to see that they all fitted perfectly. All they had to guide them were measurements. No pattern, only a picture of what we'd like. "That's skill," I told Al, when I wanted to hear more praise on our new Baghdad apparel.

Two weeks before our departure, I asked Ilyas where to find trunks. "I shall take you," he said.

On the following day he took me into the zuc under the huge dust-laden canopy. We passed the copper and tin booths where kitchen pots swung on fragile strings, small metal souvenirs of mosques and minarets, the leather sandals with rubber tire soles, British fabrics, Oriental teas, Turkish coffees, hand-made brooms and brushes. There was even a booth of Western dresses hung on American hangers. Finally I saw some tin trunks shining in a dark corner and Ilyas told me to wait. "I will buy it the trunks, Memsah," he said. "Then you are not paying it too much."

I watched from a distance. At first I didn't hear, only saw Ilyas and the merchant gesture with hands and face. Then I could hear the voices rising as their foreheads rose and fell like corrugated cardboards. The merchant's fists came down hard on the top of one of the trunks. Ilyas gave it a kick with a heavy foot. Now they were shouting, shaking fists, hunching shoulders, and finally, here came Ilyas smiling and weighted down with a tin trunk in each hand. He was triumphant as he staggered toward me. "Not worry, Memsah," he grinned widely. "We have it bery good bargain. I have it two trunks for paying it only one!" His face shone like a sun-ray when I paid him plus a healthy baksheesh.

NOW WE WERE ESPECIALLY watchful because we were seeing things for the last time: the tin-roofed movie house where bicycles were parked on the stage to avoid being stolen, where the rain on the roof in winter sounded like a game of ping-pong with glass marbles. We looked more carefully at the mosaic gold and blue magnificent designs that shone in the sun between the layers of pigeon droppings on the domes of the mosques, and I contemplated the artistry of the minarets, their lacy spires and dignified heights. The fat sheiks, would we ever forget them in their white robes and turbans, strutting to the coffee houses, puffing on their hookahs? I used to wonder who washed and ironed those enormous robes, and with what.

There was a huge division between the wealthy sheik and the thin workman who trotted about with his prayer rug ready to throw it down to pray five times a day wherever he might be, at the call from the muezzin up on the minaret. Then the workman lost himself in the words and incantations of the Koran. He prayed on his knees in the age-old ritual. We became aware again of the happy faces of the little boys and the sad staring eyes of the little girls. Something I loved to hear and listen to more carefully now was the horses' hooves on the cobbles below our bedroom window and the joyful songs of the early birds in a glowing pink morning sky before the sun rose and the world was still misty and cool. The sound of chickens scratching and chortling to one another as if quietly preparing themselves for the egg-laying business of the day.

"I'll miss Jeanne," I said to Al, looking into his tired, tired face. "We don't know each other really, but she's so gutsy and strong. She keeps her sense of humor no matter how dreadful her life becomes. I wonder if they'll ever get to America as Ali has promised." That was Jeanne's dream and I was afraid it would never happen.

"And I'll miss Naseeb," Al said, and then added, "but I bet we'll meet again somewhere." We reminisced about Naseeb's first appearance. "I know he won't stop here," Al said.

Al slumped down now when he sat, for his energy had burned out. Gone was the pep that whipped him out of bed in the morning. It was hard to see him drag himself from chore to chore. No complaints, just weariness. He had lost a lot of weight, too. It was definitely time to go home.

Ah, but the physics labs he had built from unpainted, yellow-stain walled rooms were now a triumph. Five of them remodeled, painted, equipped with all the science equipment possible to find in that faraway country. They were cheery rooms, too, functional and clean, with work tables and the stools the right height for experiments. The weeks of searching, anger, and frustration had paid off. The students, their Dean, and especially Al, felt gratified, even victorious.

Everything in front of my eyes turned yellow the morning we were to leave. I was hot, cold and weak.

"You must go to bed," Ali commanded. I was too enervated to object, even though there was still a house-load of packing to do. We had a 6:00 P.M. flight to Switzerland. Pauline burst into the room. "You OK, Mom?" All her usual hesitant manner was gone. There was a determination in her voice as she stood there waiting for a positive answer.

"I'll be fine," I mumbled, "though we may have to postpone our flight."

"Oh no we don't," she said with finality. "We're going tonight!" and she was halfway down the hall before I even tried another remark.

Pauline got to work where I had feebly left off. She sorted, disposed of who knows what, wrapped the fragile things carefully so that nothing would break going home. She collected the clothing from all our rooms, hauled bedding, books, trunks, boxes, and suitcases like a beaver before the floods, and, perfectionist that she was, roped and addressed them all neatly. Then flew into my room at about 4:00 P.M.

"All packed," she announced. "Can we go?" If I had been on my deathbed I would have assented, and she looked so happy, how could I say no? Then too, I was definitely on the mend. I simply smiled, stifled a huge sob, and nodded. She was radiant. There were Mimi and Joanie peeking in the door, big question marks on their foreheads.

"We're going!" Pauline sang out. Then I heard them running down the hall cracking the silent air with "We're going home! We're going!" I sat up in my bed and cried into a great big handkerchief.

THE HUGE MUD-SPLATTERED truck that was to take our tonnage of paraphernalia bumbled into the driveway and it created quite a stir in our neighborhood on that hot afternoon. When we staggered out under the weight of bags, suitcases, hats, purses, and of all things sweaters, it seemed as if everybody in Al Waziria was there. Just like Christmas, I thought.

Some waved because they understood what was happening. Others simply stared. There was the old dairy lady without her cow. Mr. Pudding in his white pajamas and tipsy turban. I thought of his wife safely tucked away in Turkey in her own home with her babies. I saw the henna-haired "schpint" lady without her spinach but with her five children and another on the way. There were the three wide-eyed little girls who ate scraps from our garbage can daily, and the old beggar who swallowed the pennies I had given him. I thought, with a heavy weight in my heart, all we've done for the lives of these wretched people is given them a momentary remembrance.

Jeanne braced herself. "I shall miss you terribly," she said. Then she hid her face in her handkerchief and I heard a quick sob as she disappeared with her two children, who were torn between tears and making funny faces at Mimi. I was grieved that I could not give Jeanne a goodbye hug and tell her she had been the friend who had kept me from going under throughout the year, and that I would never forget her.

Ali wore the mask of the lighthearted. "So, you will soon be picking oranges in your own backyard." He put his hand on Al's shoulder and wished him happiness—*"Insh Allah,"* he said, and then, "Salaam, Albert." I know that no matter what he said, in his heart he too felt a little empty.

Happiness sparks seemed to bounce off Pauline's face. I think she, of all of us, was the happiest to leave, but when she boarded the bus, she waved with her usual reserve. Mimi laughed and made donkey ears at everybody. Al pushed trunks around in some kind of order almost until the wheels turned. I was torn. I'd never see these friends again, and it made a void that at the moment I felt was impossible to fill.

Joanie gave Findik, the flea-bitten little dog, a long and tearful hug. No one to detick him any more, and her tears continued on down her chin as we drove away, blowing kisses to Mahal and his crew, who stood in a ragged line waving cheerily.

We waved until the dust behind the truck rose into a great cloud and hid us.

My throat contracted when I saw the crowd at the airport. The Dean, the faculty, and the students with whom Al had worked all year were there to see him off. The Dean bowed to Al graciously and gave a speech of praise and gratitude. They all bowed formally and said a final "Salaam, Doctor, and fi aman el lah." They touched their fingertips to their foreheads and their lips, then folded their hands together and bowed their heads just slightly.

Huddled together under a palm tree were my friends from Spinney's store. There was old Shaabas and his family, smiling a little sadly. Ilyas, who had been so ill, and who took care of many of our needs, stood with his six sisters dressed in their abayahs, nodding and smiling. "Fi aman el lah, Memsah," they whispered, too intimidated because of their position in life to call out. They gave special attention to Joanie and Mimi just because children are their favorite people. They honored Pauline with a more gracious bow. We touched the hands of each one, and I saw a longing in their gaze like that of prisoners warned against speaking. They must remember that they are in the low class. I ached for them as we climbed the steps and entered the great steel bird that would carry us away from the land where misery over-shadowed hope.

As we taxied slowly down the runway, I saw across a broken fence about a dozen small boys waving and laughing, jumping up and down and racing with our plane. I breathed a sigh of relief. There must always be that sound and that sight, I thought. We waved frantically, then lifted off and away.

Epilogue

Al and Joan

WAS IT A MISTAKE to pull the children out of school in Redlands in 1951 and take them to Baghdad, which, for a Western family, posed such drastic changes? Was it fair to ask Joan to give up her newly established home in exchange for the inconveniences and uncertainties of a totally foreign setting? Was it worth it? How did the experience affect our lives? Would I do it again in the light of what I now know?

These are the questions that haunt me in 1987 as I sit, alone, in my round house on the Corte Madera marsh. The very fact that I *am* alone is probably related to the Baghdad experience. But, let me explore first what I think it did for my children and my wife.

The year in Baghdad had the most devastating effects on Mimi, our youngest. She was only six when she entered the Catholic Convent school in Baghdad but she was put in the same classroom with her sister Joanie who was ten and Pauline who was thirteen. Mimi had only recently entered school in Redlands and had not yet learned to read or write. She did not know what the word "dictation" meant, so when Sister Rose asked the pupils to get ready for dictation Mimi looked around to see what the other children were doing. She took her copy book out of her desk and held her pencil in her hand the way the others did, not knowing what would come next.

Mimi was a quiet and gentle child and very pretty. She was probably the youngest and smallest girl in the class, dressed, like all the rest, in the gruesome black school uniform. I can visualize her olive skin, her black hair in bangs and her eyes of greenish tinge and I can only imagine what was in her heart into which Sister Rose had struck terror.

Sister Rose had a sadistic streak and looked down upon Americans whose education she considered inferior. Seeing Mimi fumbling she came up to her and yanked the book out from her hands causing the pencil to streak across the page. Sister Rose held the page up to the class and said, "This is the work of an American," and then to Mimi, harshly, "Sit down!"

Then Sister Rose tore the page out of Mimi's book, crumpled it up and tossed it on the floor but would not let her pick it up. She then drew a circle on the floor and told Mimi to stand inside of it as a form of punishment. She finally ordered Mimi to pick up the paper.

Mimi was terrified and humiliated. She didn't know what was going on. She told me this story recently by dictating it into a cassette tape recorder. When I listened to it in the privacy of my home I wept. As a teacher I have always felt that the most damaging thing a teacher can do is to use ridicule.

She told me one more Sister Rose story. When it was Mimi's turn to read a page from their textbook Mimi was petrified because she had never done anything like it. She simply did not know how to read. Sister Rose told her, angrily, to have her mother teach her how to read that particular page. By drilling with Mimi, Joan helped her memorize that page so that when her turn came again Mimi was able to "read" it. Then Sister Rose ordered Mimi to turn to a page she had not memorized and asked her to read that. Of course she couldn't do it and the ridicule began all over again.

To this day Mimi has difficulty with the printed word. She has never experienced the pleasure and understanding that reading can bring to people. She refused even to consider going to college because of it. She is very intelligent and has managed to learn things in other ways and to make a significant artistic and humanitarian contribution to society, but the printed page is still something she dreads in spite of conscious efforts to overcome her weakness. The joy of reading was apparently squeezed out of her life by the Baghdad experience.

Joanie suffered because she came down with hepatitis in Baghdad. Unlike Pauline and Mimi, who had been hospitalized with it in Redlands before coming to Baghdad, Joanie had to pull through it more painfully and over a much longer time interval for lack of adequate medical care. But what was probably worse, she developed a fear of eating anything that might upset her stomach and cause her to vomit. The dread of vomiting was probably worse than the act, which apparently she has never been able to consummate. Even now she speaks of "her demons"—fears which to someone else might seem unfounded but which to her have been very real and at times devastating.

Pauline told me recently that she felt she had suffered the least. She was the oldest and managed to cope well in school. She has the closest to an Anglo-Saxon appearance of anyone in our family and possibly for that reason was better liked by the British nuns in the Presentation school. Whatever bouts of illness she had must have been short-lived. I can't remember them.

Mother Joan suffered because at that time in her life she was not by nature adventuresome. She liked her comfortable little house and her pretty flower garden in Redlands and would never, of her own free will, have chosen to leave them to go to a hot and dirty place where everything was so different and so difficult, especially for a woman. Feeding, clothing, nursing, and healing each of us as we succumbed to accidents or illness was her responsibility in a situation where solutions were always difficult and sometimes impossible. She bore up under it amazingly well. Or so it seemed outwardly. But the very fact that she came down with fever and severe headaches occasionally now indicates to me that some of this must have been due to grinding stress generated by overwhelming responsibility.

After Baghdad, as the years progressed, Joan continued to go along with me as a supportive spouse and partner in my activities, but the headaches got worse and the cumulative effect of all this turmoil, reinforced by the women's liberation movement of the sixties, eventually gave Joan the courage to pick up and leave me. That's another story, but I mention it because the downward trend may have begun in Baghdad.

Now I must ask myself, "Were there any positive aspects to the Baghdad interlude?" All members of my family have told me, at one time or another, that it was an eye-opening experience and that it enriched their lives in different ways.

In her recent book Joanie says, "After one year Popsy took a job with Unesco, to teach and build a physics lab at the University of Baghdad. Perhaps that was where my passion for social justice was born." This is the woman who founded the Institute for the Study of Non-violence and later Humanitas International, a foundation devoted to civil rights world-wide.

Mimi founded and has directed for over ten years the Marin County organization called Bread and Roses, which brings free, live entertainment to people confined or isolated in institutions. Each month they present about 40 shows in hospitals, prisons, juvenile halls, convalescent homes, and centers for the disabled. I like to think that her social conscience was awakened in Baghdad. The title of her organization comes from a poem which includes these words:

"Our lives shall not be sweated from birth until life closes, hearts starve as well as bodies, give us bread and give us roses."

Possibly in rebellion to the activism of her sisters and her father, Pauline adopted a quiet lifestyle deep in the woods near Tassajara, not far from Carmel Valley. Her partner, Peyton Bryan, a skilled carpenter, built a cabin which includes a room for their daughter Pearl. On a nearby knoll Pauline built a separate little room—it's more like a doll's house — for herself, using mostly locally available or scrap materials. It displays the ingenuity and creativity which she once focused on the design of dresses in a shop which she ran until she decided the life of business was not for her.

Some would consider the Bryans' mode of living in this beautiful valley somewhat primitive, but their home is an informal social center which attracts other caring and like-minded young people. They do have some of the basic amenities such as water and electricity and a wood stove that keeps their quarters warm and cozy during winter. Pauline has a lifestyle that wastes less energy and does less harm to the environment than that of most people. By comparison, the amount of fuel used in just one of my trans-Atlantic jet hops to attend an international environmental meeting is outrageous. Who is doing more good for the environment?

After Joan left me in the 70s she joined a group of nurses who went to Somalia to set up feeding centers and medical dispensaries. She wrote a book about it called *One Bowl of Porridge*. This time she exercised her own free will and made the choice to leave house and garden to help in a distant humanitarian effort. Why did she do it? I cannot prove it, but I think the Baghdad experience may have set the stage for that move.

For me, Baghdad was a watershed. It affected the rest of my life. It enabled me to experience what it means to live in a less developed country and learn, through bitter experience, how difficult it is to effect change, especially through the mechanism of a large, bureaucratic international organization. It reinforced my belief that science and technology education have a role to play in development and that Unesco's objective of planting the seeds of peace, through education, is on the right track.

Partly because of my Baghdad experience I was invited to Unesco in Paris to come to Headquarters ten years later and head up a newly formed Division of Science Teaching. There I helped develop science teaching improvement activities such as the pilot projects in the basic sciences in Asia, Africa, Latin America, and the Arab States.

After six years in Paris with Unesco I felt I couldn't return to full-time university teaching. There seemed to be so many other more interesting things to do. I helped produce almost 100 physics teaching films for *Encyclopaedia Britannica*. I was made chairman of the Commission on the Teaching of Science of ICSU, the International Council of Scientific Unions. Later I was named Chairman of the Commission on Education of IUCN, the International Union for Conservation of Nature and Natural Resources. The operational word was "international." Baghdad had launched me on an international career. I am still invited to speak at conferences all over the world.

Was going to Baghdad worthwhile for me? Of course it was. It broadened my horizons. Would I do it over again? If circumstances were exactly as they were when I first made the decision, I would be forced to repeat it. Perhaps a more meaningful question would be, "Do you *regret* having gone to Baghdad?" To which I would respond, "I regret having caused my family pain and inconvenience. I regret that my adventure-some ways, which started with Baghdad, probably contributed to alienation between Joan and myself. But I do not regret having achieved a world view which had its start in the land of The Thousand and One Nights."

Joan

LOOKING BACK AND thinking of all the plusses and minuses of our year in Baghdad, I see how much of it enriched my life and the lives of our children. Certainly it was of great reward to Al.

True, it was hard to leave our new friends in Redlands. How generous they had been in helping us with the procedure of settling in; our collie puppy, Mr. Wooly; our fireside and peanut butter. But I'll be forever grateful to Al for such an adventure.

First of all, our dark-skinned Joanie learned that only one-quarter of the world is white and being hassled because of color, as she had been—this was Southern California—she discovered was pretty narrow minded.

Second, and important, all three girls had enough writing material stored up when we left to take care of the rest of their school years of essays.

There were hardships in Baghdad that not a youth in all this lovely state of California could possibly imagine, and though I often wondered how right we were to put our children through some of them, my one thought was that as long as we were together, we could pull through panic and pitfalls. As my British friend says, "Builds good character, that." That, meaning coping with outrageous problems.

Once, a couple of years ago, I said to one of the girls, "Tell me honestly what you think: would you rather have stayed home, been with your friends, gone to school regularly and lived a sort of normal life?"

There was no hesitation in her answer. She said almost dramatically, "And stayed in little old Redlands? God, Mummy, no!"

We surely did more than our share of griping, but seeing new scenes, new people, their strange customs, ways of living anywhere, is special for me, and what could have been more special than actually seeing what was once the Garden of Eden? Considering the whole adventure, I was, we were, lucky.

There were a few things that I will always cherish in the secret quarters of my memory; the cool and colorful early mornings; the adoring eyes of small Jamille who carried my basket through the marketplace; hearing the stories of the keepers of Spinney's store; the look on Jeanne's face when Ali presented her with the Kelvinator refrigerator, "Oh Ali," she had said, "isn't it beautiful!" She had tears in her eyes.

Best of all, even though she always called me Mrs. Baez and I know I may never see her again, she became my valued and life-long friend. Bless you, Jeanne.

ABOUT THE AUTHORS

ALBERT V. BAEZ is a renowned educator and physicist and pioneer in the field of holography. He is now president of the humanitarian foundation Vivamos Mejor/USA, and Chairman Emeritus of the Commission on Education for the International Union for Conservation of Nature and Natural Resources.

JOAN BAEZ, SR., has traveled all over the world on behalf of Friends Outside, Humanitas International, and Emergency Relief Fund International, and is the author of *One Bowl of Porridge: Memoirs of Somalia.*